SUCCESSFUL WRITING
A BEGINNER'S GUIDE

SUCCESSFUL WRITING

A BEGINNER'S GUIDE

by

JENNIE HAWTHORNE

LUTTERWORTH PRESS
GUILDFORD and LONDON

First published 1972

ISBN 0 7188 1901 2

Printed in Great Britain by
Cox & Wyman Ltd., London, Fakenham and Reading

CONTENTS

PART 1. CREATION AND MOTIVATION

Chapter   *Page*
1. WHY WRITE?   11
2. TOOLS OF THE TRADE   14
3. GETTING STARTED   19
4. IDEAS: WHAT MAKES THEM SELL?   22
5. IDEAS: WHERE TO FIND THEM   25
6. BEGINNINGS AND ENDINGS   30
7. FINDING A TITLE   35
8. LETTERS   38
9. WRITE HIGH, AIM LOW   45

PART 2. MARKETS AND MARKETING

Chapter
10. BUSINESS COMMUNICATION   57
11. ESSAY-TYPE EXAMINATIONS   62
12. FEATURES   71
13. THE RELIGIOUS PRESS   75
14. TRADE AND PROFESSIONAL MAGAZINES   81
15. THE 'GIVE-AWAY' PRESS   84
16. THE CHILDREN'S MARKET   88
17. FICTION   93
18. NON-FICTION: BOOKS   101
19. RADIO AND TELEVISION   106

Appendices
   I Layout of a Drama Script (*Notes*)   113
  II Layout of a Drama Script (Illustrated)   114
 III Notes on Writing Plays for *Television*   116
     Index   118

ACKNOWLEDGEMENTS

For some of the information on pages 12, 22, and 23, I am indebted to the *Daily Mail*, the *Sunday Express* and *The Guardian* newspapers respectively, and for the quotation from *Dossier of Medical Detection* on page 32 to publishers Victor Gollancz and author Berton Roueche.

Sources which provided help and enjoyment in the writing of this book and are not specifically mentioned in the text include: *O'Neill* by Arthur and Barbara Gelb; *Edgar Wallace: The Biography of a Phenomenon* by Margaret Lane; *The Hugo Winners* edited by Isaac Asimov (for *Flowers For Algernon* by D. Keyes); *My Brother's Keeper* by Stanislaus Joyce.

I cannot conclude any acknowledgements without mentioning my mother, Mrs. Susan Crawley, who taught me the magic of words, and Sister Hedwig, late headmistress of St. Anne's School, Whitechapel, who gave me the chance to use them.

Part One

CREATION AND MOTIVATION

CHAPTER 1

WHY WRITE?

Yᴏᴜ pick up a book entitled Sᴜᴄᴄᴇssғᴜʟ Wʀɪᴛɪɴɢ: A Bᴇɢɪɴɴᴇʀ's Gᴜɪᴅᴇ, and the first chapter is headed, Why Write? Doesn't that seem strange? But you must ask this question, otherwise you may write in vain, never achieving what you set out to do.

The aim of this book is to teach you to write successfully. But success means different things to different people. You may want to be read by associates on the Board of Directors or workers on the shop floor. You may want your writing to be read and responded to in the most desirable way by your beloved. You may want to write a novel, or a poem; to be published by a certain magazine or newspaper; to persuade an employer that you are the only man or woman for the job he offers; or to persuade a mass market that your product is the only one of its kind worth buying. You may want your writing to be marked in the most rewarding though not necessarily deserving manner by the examiner surveying the results of your long years of study or lack of them.

These aims can be summed up under five headings: writing for pleasure, payment, publication, prestige and response. The pleasure may arise from receiving a cheque for your writing or having it published without any payment at all, from seeing your work discussed in a learned magazine or merely getting a reply to a letter. In all these cases the pleasure comes as a result of being successful in what you set out to do . . . in achieving your aim: getting paid, or published, gaining prestige or response.

But pleasure can also be unadulterated, springing from the writing act itself without thought of payment, publication, prestige or response. It is a kind of joy in communicating, in formulating abstract or complex ideas into intelligible prose, in wrestling with words to construct a medley of sense and sound that has, for the writer at least, a ring of harmony or truth or both. Yet even people who get happiness in this way sometimes have a sneaking desire for publication.

I was once asked to help a person who had been writing for twenty years without having anything published. It seemed absolutely incredible to me that an intelligent man holding down a responsible job should have continued writing for so long without ever having had a word published, though he had sent his work out. What motivated him? What made him on most nights of the week, isolate himself away from his family in a little upstairs room for the toil of writing unpublishable novels? I don't know. He must have got some joy from the exercise, but after twenty years even this proved insufficient reward.

He showed me a novel he had written. I put him on to a market. Six months later the novel was accepted. Though the writer has never made the headlines, five more published novels have since come from his pen, an average of one a year since his first 'success'. So this story had a happy ending.

But there are thousands of people for whom acceptance never comes. They write novels, short stories, articles and poems that never find a publisher. Mrs. Pat Townsend, a Buckinghamshire housewife, started writing when she was twenty-eight years old. She has turned out 100,000 words in articles, short stories and poetry and, in her own words, "spent a fortune on writers' magazines and correspondence courses" without having a word published. But she keeps on trying. Like most writers she finds that "it's something I can't help doing".

Tony Joseph, a Bristol librarian, started writing when he was twenty-eight as a hobby. He has written a biography of 120,000 words, a novel of 43,000 words rejected by eight publishers, and is beginning a second. He has had a few articles published about his work, but it is not these successes which make him go on. Like Mrs. Townsend, he says: "It's something inside me. Even if I still don't get anywhere, I'll keep on writing."

Sylvia Anderson, a Middlesex nurse and housewife, has collected fifty publishers' rejection slips. A 75,000 word novel she completed took ten years' intermittent work. Rewritten nine times, it resulted in a total output of about one million words . . . with no publisher.

All these—so far—unsuccessful writers have the very necessary quality of staying power.

But writing without a single acceptance would for many people be sheer purgatory, and they would give up long before ten—or twenty—

years. Some would not survive a year. So it is wise before you start writing to analyse why you want to do so.

For most people, the usual answer is publication. They want the satisfaction of their name in print, their ideas communicated. For other writers, publication is not enough. They want payment not only as a reward for their labours but because payment gives a basis of comparison and proves that their work has value in a very competitive market place.

Another reason for attempting to write is prestige. To be published in certain magazines is a form of professional success. It is often considered to be a mark of distinction, like getting a Ph.D. for writing a thesis, though the thesis may be commercially unpublishable. Publication in certain magazines can be an aid to a person's career, and the prestige of appearing in these learned journals is therefore more important than the far higher payment in a popular magazine or mass circulation newspaper.

Many years ago I had my first acceptance by *The Guardian*. The prestige of being published by that paper seemed to me to be an achievement beside which the writing of a novel was a mere trifle. Today I usually put payment as my first priority, although if I were trying to raise support for a cause or to remedy an injustice, publication would, in this case, be far more important than any payment.

Lastly, there is writing for response. In other words, writing to make people respond in the way you want them to: writing to get interviewed for a job; to give instructions which must be carried out; writing examination answers to get maximum marks, writing a letter to a newspaper or an M.P., to a charity in order to attract funds for a good cause, or to an organization or even a parent asking for financial help. You don't want to spend money on a telegram to your father saying "No mon, no fun, your son" to get back the reply "How sad, too bad, your Dad."

So before you start writing at all, ask yourself why you are doing it. What is your aim? Having defined your aim you can then move on to the next important step of achieving it.

CHAPTER 2

TOOLS OF THE TRADE

FIRST of all, let us deal with writing for publication. If your work is not published in some form it will not be responded to or paid for. Neither will it earn any prestige. And to get work published you need tools.

"All your material is in your mind", aspirant writers are sometimes told when they start off on what they hope is the beginning of a new career. "You don't need any tools." Such advice may have been good enough for the Brontë sisters, for Dickens, Thackeray or Scott, but the typewriter has now been invented, and even Len Deighton who declares a writer needs only a pen and pad, uses an I.B.M. computerized typewriter for his own output.

The genius or person of great talent might get a publisher's loving welcome for his handwritten manuscript, but geniuses, of whom there are very few, will find it easier still to get work accepted when it is easy to read. As for the non-genius sending in a handwritten manuscript, 99 times out of a 100 all he will get is a rejection slip.

So after a pencil and pad for jotting down ideas, the first tool of the trade for most people is a typewriter. This does not mean vast expense. On the contrary, manuscripts can be expertly typed for a small fee. Even the loan of an expensive electric typewriter costs less than £6 per month and nearly half of that is an allowable tax expense. Other tools are a book of quotations; an encyclopaedia for looking up facts, current events, centenaries and topical dates; an atlas and any similar aid to accuracy in your work.

If your grammar, spelling or vocabulary is weak, do something about it. Monica Dickens once told me in an interview I had with her that if a writer's ideas were sufficiently creative, editors would buy their work even if it had spelling errors or badly expressed ideas. Anybody, she declared, could correct spelling and grammar. Comparatively few could create. This picture seems to present too rosy a view of the writing world.

A highly creative and readable writer might get a book with incorrect syntax, spelling and grammar, accepted. Editors assure me, however, that manuscripts are quite often rejected on these grounds alone in spite of possessing colourful and original ideas.

So, if you are in this class of original creative thinkers who spell badly, make errors of syntax and grammar, a remedial English book should be one of your tools of the trade, together with some novels or short stories by skilled practitioners in the art of writing, whom you enjoy reading and whose work can serve you as a model.

Buy a dictionary and never write a word the spelling or meaning of which you are uncertain. Look it up. *Modern English Usage* by Fowler can help the educated reader and writer on tricky points of language usage but will not be so helpful for the average person who wants to improve his grammar or spelling. Every library and bookseller, however, stocks some books the aim of which is to improve the writer's grammatical skills. Choose one that suits *you*.

Alternatively, you might be able to find an agent who, for a fee, will bring your MS. up to publication standard. A list can be found in *The Writers' and Artists' Year Book*, which is mentioned below.

Market guides give some idea of outlets and payment for what you write. The best one for the beginner is *The Writers' and Artists' Year Book*, revised annually, which lists some 100 Sunday and daily newspapers, 1,000 weekly ones and 2,000 general magazines. It also has other useful sections on overseas publications, British and foreign publishers, literary agents and awards; and a journalist's calendar. *Willing's Press Guide* with addresses of all the major newspapers in the world and their circulation figures, is another source of markets. *Benn's Newspaper Directory* is the most monumental of them all, listing all kinds of journals published throughout the world, including house journals and professional magazines. There is also *British Rate and Data*, used a great deal by advertising media because it lists the charges for advertising space and William Dawson's *Little Red Book Guide to the Free Press of The World Subscription Prices*, which gives the cost of an annual subscription to any of more than 100,000 magazines listed in alphabetical order within its compact format.

The American scene is most ably represented by *Writer's Market,* edited by Kirk Polking and Natalie Hagan. A fairly substantial tome of around 700 pages and costing about $9, it provides details of 4,000 markets for the freelance writer.

With the exception of the last two, these market guides are available in most public libraries, so the impoverished beginner need not complain that he has no money to buy them. The library will also provide a desk, chair and quiet in the reference room, so he cannot complain about noise or lack of facilities either.

A personal file of press cuttings saves travelling to town centres to look up current information. Use a cardboard box divided into subject headings or you can buy concertina-type cardboard files which fold flat, for under £1.50 at most stationers. Into this subject file put press clippings and in theory you should be able to turn out a factual article instantly when anything topical or newsworthy on your file subjects crops up.

Business Surveys, Ltd., of The Mead, Wallington, provide a fortnightly source list of topics from aeronautics to zoology based on daily and weekly newspapers. Subscriptions cost £35 per annum, too expensive for the beginner, but copies are available or can be obtained for you in the public libraries. Such sources and your own files give the most up-to-date information which cannot always be obtained from text books. I like, too, the *Guinness Book of Records*, not only for the vast amount of odd and interesting facts it contains, but for the endearing anecdotal quality with which it relates them.

A tape recorder or dictating machine increases output and the resultant tape can easily be typed by the writer or a helpful friend at a later date. I use a Philips Portable Tape Recorder because it is so light and trouble free. The cassettes give up to one hour each side, playing time.

These are some of the tangible tools of the trade. There are also what may be termed, intangible tools or qualities a writer needs in order to succeed. The most important is persistence. For many years, I have taught adults in Education Centres courses on Creative Writing. Most of my students have been successful in one way or another in their work, but the most successful have not always had more talent than the rest. They had more persistence. They continued pushing out work when the others merely thought about it or only got half way through a piece or received one or two rejections and then gave up.

Yet why should anybody, even a genius, assume writing success is going to come easily? Until he was forty years of age, Bernard Shaw never earned more than £5 from any of his books. "I doubt whether any living novelist can show such a record", he wrote. John Creasey, author of more than 300 books, who gets £1,000 advance for his thrillers, had over 700 rejections before his first sale.

Alan Sillitoe's *Saturday Night and Sunday Morning* has now achieved the distinction of being almost compulsory reading for English Literature courses. Yet it was rejected by twelve publishers before W. H. Allen took it. R. J. Delderfield completed five novels and many short stories, all rejected before he penned *Worm's Eye View*, which ran for more than 2,000 performances and earned him £30,000. Thackeray's *Vanity Fair* was turned down many times, and a publisher wrote of Proust's masterpiece, *Remembrance of Things Past*, that he could not see why twelve pages were necessary to describe how a person turned round in bed before going to sleep.

So persistence you must have ... and it pays. It is necessary to emphasize this, as the following story shows. A friendly editor offered me some space in his journal and I passed on the market to my students, any one of whom with a little effort could have been assured of publication at the very respectable rate for beginners of £4.20 per 500 words. They had 'no time', were doing odd jobs, housework, etc., and only one actually got down to the task of writing.

Within months she had established herself, and was earning some regular pocket money. She also became the paper's Gourmet Columnist, going out with her husband to dine and wine in restaurants free of charge, and writing up the experience in the paper. The money she earned from her writing in one year covered her course fee over one hundred times.

Secondly, after persistence, there must be a feeling for words, a liveliness of ideas or freshness of outlook; some expertise or passion, an originality of thought or dialogue, something at least that can be polished and burnished until it shines through for all to recognize as talent.

The third quality needed for success is organization. Without organization you are never going to reap high rewards from writing or from much else either. Organization is a technique which can be learnt, or, when you are rich, delegated. In the beginning, however, you must keep records of work you have sent out, its success or rejection and editor's comment, if any, together with details of all payments received. These records will help you analyse your most profitable markets and will ease your relations with the Inland Revenue.

If you deal in facts you must know where to find them, and be able to record them accurately. I read somewhere that proof readers who checked copy for an American news magazine had to place a dot over every word of the copy to show that it had been checked. Freelance beginners should have similarly high aims, even if there is an occasional fall from grace.

All right, I can hear you say, impatiently. I have got my typewriter, paper, dictionaries, even my tape recorder. I'm sure I don't lack talent. I'm going to be accurate, very well organized and incredibly persistent. But how do I *start*?

CHAPTER 3

GETTING STARTED

SOME people are self motivating. They are so full of ideas that they cannot help creating articles and stories. They need no tips on getting started.

Erle Stanley Gardner, creator of the Perry Mason series, turned out in May, 1931, eleven stories, an output of 132,000 words. Another American, Mark Hellinger, used to write and sell one short story every day.

Charles Hamilton (Frank Richards) who created Greyfriars School and Billy Bunter, weekly wrote 80,000 words for the comics *Gem* and *Magnet*. Georges Simenon produces twenty pages of a novel in a day. His current total output of 500 books is exceeded only by the inimitable John Creasey. Women writers (and readers) may not be so impressed by Simenon's daily production of twenty pages when they learn that his children's playroom is soundproofed. A greater feat in some ways might be the novels of Maria Edgeworth who wrote with over twenty step-sisters and stepbrothers in the house.

In his speed of writing, Nat Gould was almost as fast as the horses about which he so often wrote. He used to produce in longhand, a novel of 60,000 words in a fortnight. When he died in 1919, twenty-two of his books awaited publication. They earned a fortune for his heirs.

Such prolific writers as these need no help on getting started. But for others the sight of a sheet of blank paper has the most stultifying effect. It drains them of ideas and paralyses their faculties to such an extent they cannot put a single word down on paper.

There are two remedies for this inactivity. One is to keep a notebook in a locker or handbag over the kitchen sink, on the desk or what serves as a desk . . . anywhere that is easily accessible each day. Jot down ideas, incidents, descriptions of people, anything that comes into your head.

If your mind still seems blank, put down children's sayings. It is almost impossible for a day to go by without toddlers saying something that amuses an adult. Comment on happenings at work, at home, in the street, the shops, on the book you are currently reading, the state of the garden, the house, the office. If all else fails and you find it absolutely impossible to make any notes at all, then see how others have compiled their jottings. Read Somerset Maugham's *Writer's Notebook* or look through a current newspaper or the requirements listed in the *Writers' and Artists' Year Book* to see what editors want.

Analyse at the end of each day the notes you have written down and see if any of them can be made into an article, story or letter for the press.

Ask yourself who will be interested, who cares? Writing out an article, poem or story without an audience in mind may be fun. But why should an editor publish the piece if it has no relevance or interest for his readers? He, and they, want their fun, too.

Even if the ideas in your notebook appear trivial, remember that most people do not lead lives of great moment except to themselves. Apparently trivial ideas can turn into saleable articles.

During a period when I had four young children at home, I sold articles on Dustbins to *Municipal Engineering*, on Baby Feeding and associated subjects to *Parents, Nursing Mirror* and *Mother*; on Sweeping-up the Bedroom to *The Guardian*, on Family Outings and Christenings to the *Birmingham Post* and *Catholic Herald*. Nobody, however charitable, would call these world-shattering subjects, but they sold and brought in welcome pin money when there was no other way of earning it.

I would have liked to have produced stories or a good novel, but four children may have been a big enough effort of creation in themselves. We were a Service family, constantly on the move, eleven times in almost as many years. It is disconcerting to start a story, move home, and then almost before one has unpacked and recalled the hero and heroine to mind, to have to search for or be 'posted' to a new address. I lacked the creativity of the real author in these circumstances and found it easier turning out small pieces which could be started and quickly completed anywhere.

Within a year of my husband's leaving the Service and buying our own home, I did write a children's novel. I was then forty-one and expecting my seventh child. The book was accepted by the first publisher to whom it was submitted.

So do not despise the so-called trivial ideas. Written up in attractive or controversial guise they will prove a valuable form of apprenticeship. They will teach you many aspects of writing skill, help you achieve continuous sales and maybe in time to come, who knows?—the jackpot rewards of the best-seller market.

After the ideas notebook, the second aid to starting is discipline. Make yourself a certain time, if not every day, then every other day, or every third day, when you will write. Don't use the old excuse, 'no time'. All time is allocated between the things you want to do and those you must. Fortunate is the man for whom 'must' and 'want' are the same; wise is the man who knows the difference and acts on it.

If all else fails, carve out time in the early morning hours. Mrs. Kay Thorpe, author of *Opportune Marriage* and other romantic novels, wrote in the evenings and once a week all through the night from 8 p.m. to 4 a.m. to produce four novels in eighteen months.

Arnold Bennett rose at 5.30 a.m. and began work at 6 a.m. which enabled him in 1899 to complete 200 articles and short stories, an output of 330,000 words. So find time somehow. Sit down with your ideas pad and *start writing*.

CHAPTER 4

IDEAS: WHAT MAKES THEM SELL?

"I've got a whole lot of ideas in my notebook, but who's going to buy them?" the beginner may well ask when at the end of the day he looks at the collection of jottings he has made. The answer is simple. Ideas for articles and stories become publishable if and when they meet the needs of a reader.

You may sum up the readers' needs in whatever fashion you please. But the easiest grouping is to make five main headings. (*a*) *Spiritual*: the need to worship, to find an acceptable basis for living (read Alexander Zolzhenitsyn's *Cancer Ward* to see how the question, by what standards does a man live, is answered). (*b*) *Mental*: education, the desire to learn; crafts, hobbies, skills. (*c*) *Social*: human relationships, work, love, marriage, parentcraft, environment. (*d*) *Physical*: understanding and care of the body; sex, food, sport, shelter, security. (*e*) *Emotional*: the craving for romance, amusement; the interest in conflict and mystery.

If any of your ideas can be geared to meet these five types of human needs, you are well on the way to a publishable story, article, book.

Harold Robbins, one of the highest paid living novelists, estimates that his writing has earned him over £8 million in 23 years. How did he make it? In his own words, "I'm the best writer around. The trouble with too many writers is they remove themselves to a literary world and they start writing to impress other writers or the critics. But that's not what it's about. It's to get to people."

"Selling books like *The Carpet Baggers* or *The Adventurers* is easy", you may retort. But other writers producing different work get equally high sales.

Alistair MacLean, author of *The Guns of Navarone*, explains his writing philosophy. "I'm not a novelist . . . I'm a story teller, that's all. It's a job like any other. The secret, if there is one, is speed. That's why there's so little sex in my books. It holds up the action." Yet without sex in his books and relying on plot, pace and action, he earns over £200,000 annually, selling in Britain alone, 2,750,000 books in hard cover and eight million in paperback. Agatha Christie and Georges Simenon, also in the best selling league, appeal to the need in a reader for entertainment, mystery, conflict.

Mary Stewart, clergyman's daughter, former University Lecturer in English and wife of a Professor of Geology, has paperback sales in America topping eight million. Her stories have a background of glamour. The heroines are usually about 25, pretty and intelligent. The heroes are a little older and charming. With these elements as part of her formula for writing romantic thrillers, she sells 60,000 copies of every new book she writes.

Romance is a booming industry for publishers as well as writers. Mills and Boon produce 144 in hardback every year. Dr. Peter H. Mann discovered from a survey of 2,788 readers that they are read by age groups from 15 upwards, not only by older women as had been thought. One reader said her husband had built two cupboards to house her collection of 500 books; a hairdresser declared she went without nylons to buy her romances and a 91-year old nurse claimed to have read 791 Mills and Boon romances and liked all but one.

On a lesser plane why will editors pay fees ranging from a mere £2 up to £50 for 1,000 words, and for a series, amounts veering from £500 to £25,000? The answer is reader appeal.

For articles (unlike stories), reader appeal needs to be backed up by facts. Not always ... you may be so full of passion and fire that your piece gets published simply as an idea because it will arouse controversy and therefore interest in readers. Not always ... you may be so talented or gifted a writer that you will be in demand for 'think pieces' alone. But if you are not a humorist, or a naturally gifted writer and want to achieve consistent sales, you will need facts to prove your case, to illustrate the points you are trying to make.

Another important element in a saleable idea is slant. To whom does your idea appeal? How many people are likely to be interested? If the answer is only a few, then you will have to search diligently for a publisher. The more universal the appeal, the easier will the idea or story be to sell, for there is a wider audience. An article, however well-written, about walking, has a far more limited magazine audience than an article about drivers, driving or cars. Walkers do not pay for magazine adverts. Car manufacturers do.

Write about parish pump affairs and your outlets will be a small handful of church news letters. Write about sex education and, currently, many more readers will be interested in your work.

Slant means writing to suit particular market needs; placing your ideas where they have some special significance or point for the reader. As an example of slanting, I once wrote down the idea 'Crammers', being interested at the time in fee-paying schools and institutions which helped students pass certain exams. I turned out a very good piece called '*Tutors, Inc,*' yet it was rejected by a dozen markets. Because I had faith in the quality of the article, I sent it on the thirteenth occasion to *The Tatler*, a socialite magazine. They paid me what was then the very good rate of £26 per 1,000 words. Had the piece been accepted by one of the earlier papers to which it had gone, I would have been lucky to have got £10.

Slant or angle was the reason for its final acceptance and earlier refusals. The readership of *The Tatler* was a rich one, people interested in all aspects of good living. They could afford, if they wished, to pay expensive fees for children's education, so the descriptions of the establishments, timetables and principals I mentioned in the article, had a particular significance or appeal for the readers. An easy way of testing the 'slant' of a magazine, its leanings, is to look at the advertisements. They give a good idea of the paper's readership, and what interests them.

Summing up, then, ideas become saleable if firstly they appeal to basic needs; if, in the case of articles, they are backed up by facts, and finally if they are slanted to a market where they have a particular significance, point, or appeal.

CHAPTER 5

IDEAS: WHERE TO FIND THEM

"THERE is a time to reap and a time to sow", says the Bible. Sowing and reaping time applies to writers too, but whereas reaping time shows itself in the form of a cheque or a published article, the sowing time is hard to recognize. It may be a period of inactivity or worse still, sterility, when ideas refuse to come. Every article or story sent out, returns. The novel which has taken two years to complete, finds no publisher. Take heart. Such sterile periods are often a prelude to, or result of, productive energy.

Not everybody can have the stupendous creativity of Walter Scott, writing the 150,000 word *Guy Mannering* in just six weeks and so managing to pay off debts of £4,000. Scott eventually wrote himself into his grave paying off debts, so from the point of view of an author's self preservation, such lack of creativity may be just as well.

Dickens in his later years could not keep up with the normal 3,000–4,000 daily output of his youth and would wander round the streets of London unable to write a word.

Why then should a beginner expect to have a never-ending flow of ideas? Even the man who makes his living by his pen has days and weeks of non-production. They need not be an agonizing period of frustration, for this is the time to go out, renew acquaintances, see new sights and in this way find ideas for future sales and renew creative energy; in other words, a time to sow.

During the months when Agatha Christie writes nothing, her brain mulls over plots which eventually come to fruition in a new book to delight her 350 million readers. The beginner, too, can use his non-writing periods to observe the world more closely, to increase his knowledge by wider reading, by taking up new pastimes. He can find inspiration and motivation from joining evening classes, writers' circles, looking through magazines and noting the contents.

Public Relations officers of private firms and public corporations will

25

give him all manner of free material about services and products they are marketing, and so provide at least the facts for an article if not the will-power to write it.

Chance observations, particularly of the outdoor scene, are often the starting point of stories and features. So is the Calendar: with its anniversaries or centenaries of famous people or the cycles and seasons of the year, Easter, Christmas, autumn, spring.

A holiday can spark off new ideas, and it should result in at least one article about expensive and inexpensive ways of spending a vacation, with costs, routes, and interesting places in the area tabulated or described.

I gave an exercise to a group of students on one occasion: to write about a holiday for different sections of the reading public; a very rich group such as might be readers of *Playboy*; and a very poor group. In every case the students had to put at the beginning of their exercise the market for which they were writing. This proved a tremendously useful and profitable exercise. One student sold his very first piece to *The Times Educational Supplement* on "What the Holiday Brochures Never Reveal", a hilarious account of the mishaps which befell the leader of a school touring party overseas. Another sold an article to *The Lady* on an inexpensive cruise around the Isles of Scotland. A third gave help to young families who had to spend their holidays at home: this was published in the local newspaper; a fourth student got a column published in the Woman's Page of *Daily Telegraph* about the enforced holidays of retirement and how to make the most of them. Timing is very important for travel and holiday articles. . . . Christmas, January and Easter being the main advertising months, with the bulk in January.

Beginners are often told to "write about what you know". Such advice has certainly paid off for Margaret Powell. Her book *Below Stairs* and its sequels based on her experiences as a housemaid have brought her constant TV appearances as well as paperback fame. Similarly *I Bought a Mountain* by Thomas Firbank gives the tale of a real-life experience of a man who bought a sheep farm in the remote hillsides of Wales.

A particularly rewarding source of saleable ideas and a pleasure in itself is a visit to a museum or similar institution. One of my children wanted, on a half term holiday, to visit the Public Records Office in London. This has a museum, little known and infrequently visited, which is open to the public every afternoon to 4 p.m. Beneath its roof are stored treaties, wills, letters, public records and documents of all kinds including the Domesday Book and other material relating to historical events and personages.

While there I was very surprised to see that Karl Marx, author of the Communist Manifesto was a shareholder in the newspaper organization which he and his friends had probably set up to propagate their ideas in print and share out the resultant rewards. Marx had signed for five shares in the venture, a singularly interesting and unknown sidelight on the character of a great polemic writer.

In this museum, too, is a letter from Catherine Howard, fifth wife of Henry VIII, to Thomas Culpepper which, used as evidence of adultery and treason, caused them to be executed. It seemed such a pathetic little letter asking after the young man's health, and yet two lives were lost partly because of it (though Cranmer helped!).

Another stimulating place to visit is the Victoria and Albert Museum for fine art collections, silverware, furniture of all kinds. Look at the embroidered bed hangings worked by Mary Queen of Scots and the Countess of Bessborough. The cross stitch panels are copied from an animal drawing in a book written by Conrad Gesner in 1560. The elephant has a strange appearance because Gesner had never seen one and had only had it described to him. How long would it take a friend to recognize an elephant from your description? How well would he draw it?

To do justice to the British Museum, another source for articles, stories and books, is quite impossible in one visit. This great institution houses more than six million books, a wonderful collection of antiquities from all over the world, and of prints and drawings by such famous artists as Leonardo da Vinci and Rembrandt.

Try the Manuscript Room for a start. Look at Scott's *Kenilworth* with its careful, beautiful writing, and by contrast, the original manuscript of James Joyce's *Finnegan's Wake*, with its red crossings out and whole pieces of dialogue rephrased. Look also at Leonardo da Vinci's notebook with its neat writing and skilful diagrams, or the manuscript of *Alice in Wonderland* by Lewis Carroll with its fine layout, the clever way the words to the right of the drawing of Alice have been written without any cramping.

See the fair copy of Gray's *Elegy in a Country Churchyard* or the handwriting of Robert Burns whose father was a farmworker; the copy of a letter written by John Keats to his sister, the one by Nelson to Lady Hamilton, or the last shaky words in Captain Scott's Diary: "For God's sake, look after our people."

As a change from manuscripts, walk round the Anglo-Saxon room, with fascinating relics from the past, such as the Sutton Hoo Burial Treasure; the Ecclesiastical History of England in the case marked Chronicles of England, 1. In the adjoining case are the Lindisfarne Gospels written about A.D. 698 with each page copied out beautifully by hand and illustrated in colour, a real lesson for any of us who want to reach perfection in the art of the written word.

To visit the British Museum Coin Collection—and coin collecting is of interest to a growing number of people today—you will have to show some credentials before being admitted behind the heavy door. While you study the show cases it will be locked behind you.

For persons interested in modern art, the Tate Gallery is a better bet. Other museums which cannot fail to provide a source of inspiration for writers are: the Science Museum, the Geological, the Natural History, the London, and the small museum at Bethnal Green with its treasure of dolls, dolls houses and domestic costume. Not far away in Shoreditch is the Geffrye Museum and a modern room furnished in contemporary style. The Geffrye Museum makes an ideal outing for young people. Cut-out books and leaflets can be bought in the entrance and pencils borrowed for drawing or making notes. No excuse whatsoever here for not being able to put something down on paper!

Or there is Hampton Court, very easily accessible by all forms of transport including boat. Look at the bills and accounts of Henry VIII's household, and compare the cost of a few prayer books at over £30 with today's prices ... or candles ... or a bed. See the wonderful collection of Italian paintings, the views of the long walk and the fountain from the State drawing room. Go in Spring and enjoy the splash of colour in the gardens, the scent of the 200-year-old wistaria tree outside the vinery—which also blooms in Autumn.

Walk round the great kitchens and think of the people who once dined in the banqueting halls, or worshipped in the chapel. Finish off the day with a return trip along the Thames to London, and if you can't get one saleable idea from a day's outing like this, it's going to take a real lot of hard work to make you into a writer.

I have described in the briefest possible way some of the stimulating places of interest London and its environs have to offer. But in every country there are scenes of beauty; ancient houses and palaces with their tales of long ago. Visitors view them to delight in their history, their setting, their glory. For writers they can provide a source of inspiration for many months and even years to come.

CHAPTER 6

BEGINNINGS AND ENDINGS

THE hardest part of any writing is the beginning. From the ideas you have jotted down, you have to create a story, a character, a plot, a feature article. Anthony Trollope believed that a writer should approach his work in the same way as did any other craftsman. There should be no waiting for inspiration or any other gimmick. The writer should get on with his trade during set hours like any other worker.

Perhaps Trollope derived this attitude from his wonderful mother, Frances, who began writing at the age of fifty. Starting at 4 a.m. each day she produced thirty novels in the next twenty-six years.

Trollope's method was to plan the number of words in his novel, then apportion so many words per day to write, usually 1,000, with a watch before him to keep him from being sluggish. "The author can sit down with a pen in his hand, write for a given time and produce a certain number of words. That is comparatively easy," he said. "But to . . . turn it all in your thoughts and make things fit . . . that requires elbow grease of the mind."

Few beginners can adopt such a professional attitude to writing but they can certainly borrow Trollope's technique. The job is to write, so the first thing to do is to write, write anything at all that comes into your mind. Gradually you will find yourself able to create and construct. Like an unresponsive car engine on a cold morning you make take a long time to warm up. But unlike the car engine, the effort to get started pays dividends next time you begin. Creation and construction will become almost automatic, though a great deal of revision may have to be done before you are satisfied with your work.

If all else fails on the first occasion, use the reporting technique of WHO, WHAT, WHERE, WHEN, WHY, HOW. Who are you talking about? However fleeting his appearance, make him real for the reader. You do not have to describe him with a personal inventory. A couple of words of dialogue can reveal his background, country, even race or religion. One verb can describe his physical characteristics . . . there is a big difference between 'he strode' and 'he limped'; between 'he cringed before the blow" and 'he stood up to the blow'.

Secondly, WHO also refers to your reader. For *whom* are you writing? More will be said about the reader in Part Two on Marketing, but for the moment remember that it is a particular kind of reader buying a particular kind of magazine, newspaper, or book; a particular kind of listener or viewer that you are writing for. Speak to him in his own language. Don't talk down or up. He's not interested in technical jargon unless it's vital to the understanding of the story or feature. He wants to be entertained, informed, inspired, *moved*.

The key word WHAT means what are you saying, trying to get over? What is your point? Give facts to support your opinions, and examples that can be readily appreciated by your readers. Then WHERE did the happenings, the events take place? This element of where can be particularly important in books, for the background alone can attract the reader. Rumer Godden's *The Greengage Summer* gives a beautifully evocative atmosphere of the French countryside burgeoning into fruition, while the teenage children grow into adulthood.

. The setting of a story not only provides an element of glamour or adventure missing in real life: it is the breeding ground of the plot, the action, the characters. They could not come to life elsewhere. Look at *Brighton Rock* with its wonderfully described atmosphere of seedy horse-racing gangs at Brighton; Ring Lardner's baseball and fighting champs: see James Joyce's Dublin through the eyes of a young man; or Henry James's Europe—best of all: study the apparently innocuous setting of that wonderful horror story, *The Turn of the Screw*. The article writer is not expounding a narrative but an idea or sequence of ideas. Nevertheless he can borrow the story writer's technique in remembering the WHERE element.

WHEN can be another beginning point. When did these events take place, when did the facts which you are relating, happen? Start off with the date, if you must, to put the reader immediately into the picture, and give them the time of day or season of the year. From *Dossier of Medical Detection* by Berton Roueche, published in England by Victor Gollancz, here is the opening paragraph of the first story, *A Man Named Hoffman*.

Around ten o'clock on the morning of Wednesday, March 4, 1964, a man named Donald Hoffman presented himself for treatment at the Student Health Clinic of Miami University in Oxford, Ohio, some thirty miles northwest of Cincinnati. Hoffman was thirty-six years old, married, and a resident of Cincinnati, but, as he explained to the receptionist, he was currently employed as an insulation installer, in Oxford—on a remodeling job at McCullough-Hyde Memorial Hospital—and his company had an arrangement with the clinic. He was here, he added, because his foreman had sent him. That was the only reason. His trouble was nothing—an itchy sore on the side of his neck. He had probably picked up a sliver of glass-wool fiber. It had happened several times before. It was a common complaint in his trade.

This is an introduction to a narrative on a rare case of anthrax in the United States. But note the brilliant introduction, the narrative style, the reporting technique. See how the WHO, WHEN, WHERE, and WHAT elements are all involved.

Read the first lines of *The Outsider* by Albert Camus. Does it not also use all the WHO, WHEN, WHAT, WHERE techniques? *Who* (mother), *When* (yesterday/today?) *What* (death of) *Where* (the Home). Here is another example from that model of short story tellers, Saki. Fittingly enough, it is called, *The Story Teller*, and this is the opening:

It was a hot afternoon, and the railway carriage was correspondingly sultry, and the next stop was at Templecombe, nearly an hour ahead.

The occupants of the carriage were a small girl, and a smaller girl, and a small boy. An aunt belonging to the children occupied one corner seat, and the farther corner seat on the opposite side was occupied by a bachelor who was a stranger to their party, but the small girls and the small boy emphatically occupied the compartment.

Both the aunt and the children were conversational in a limited, persistent way, reminding one of the attentions of a housefly that refused to be discouraged. . . .

Doesn't that opening succinctly describe the setting, the people and the situation? Doesn't it use the principles, WHO, WHAT, WHEN, WHERE?

WHY and HOW of course come later. WHY did these events take place? Why are you telling the reader about them? From a novelist's or storyteller's point of view, WHY and HOW are the most crucial points of the narrative. They provide suspense and keep the reader glued to his book. He wants to find out why and how the thing was done and by whom. From the point of view of an article, why can be the passion which motivates the writer ... why he is giving you this information, or trying to convert you to his way of thinking so that you conclude his article by saying *Why not?*

This then is one useful technique of getting started, the WHO, WHEN, WHAT, WHERE technique, supplemented when necessary by WHY and HOW.

Another is the LOOK, YOU, SEE, SO.

LOOK means finding an opening which will practically stun your reader in the first line. When, not being an editor, you write anything for publication, you have a two-fold sales task: to convince an editor that your work is worth publishing and a reader that it is worth reading. All your sales efforts must therefore be concentrated in the opening lines. If the early paragraphs are dull, if they do not immediately make an impact, if they do not immediately hold and capture your audience, then unless you are writing a very long book, or have already made your name, you are finished.

LOOK means drawing the attention of the reader to what you are saying. But the opening must be relevant to the rest of the piece. It is no use writing for an article entitled SLAUGHTER ON THE ROADS, that 1 in 14 children under 16 years of age dies on the roads each year, and then going on to discuss infant mortality or diabetes or some similar irrelevancy. LOOK means look at this particular piece of information, the most arresting or significant in the whole article.

YOU comes next. The angle here is to make the information given seem particularly relevant for the reader. The reader must listen, digest and act because the material has been especially written with him in mind.

SEE is showing the proof of what you say; giving facts to back up your case. See, this cannot be gainsaid. See, this X-ray shows what cigarette smoking does to a lung. See, these statistics prove how true my argument is.

SO ties up the ending and brings it to a successful close which is what I hope soon to do with this chapter. It is usually of two types: a summary emphasizing the main points of the story and which repeats the theme expounded in the first paragraph; or it may be a sequel, a twist ending like one of O. Henry's stories, or a paragraph which completes the piece in so dramatic or unexpected a way, or one that is so completely satisfying that the reader cannot put the piece down unmoved. Read the last line in *Brighton Rock*. There cannot be a better ending to such a story than that, can there?

CHAPTER 7

FINDING A TITLE

THE first aim of a title is to draw and hold a reader. It is a form of advertising, a device to capture an audience. But it would be unfair on the reader to have a title like, "How I Survived Twenty Years in the Desert", if when he opened the book or read through the article there was nothing about the desert as it is commonly understood, or about survival either. He would feel let down, deceived. The second aim of the title must therefore be to summarize the theme; to give in a few eye-catching words the main idea of the article, the crux of the story.

Thus a story entitled, "A Cool Way to Commit a Murder", suggests to the reader the idea of a crime or detective story. Alistair MacLan's *The Guns of Navarone* must be an adventure, and Wilkie Collins already indicates in the title of his *The Woman in White* that suggestion of mystery which the ingeniously plotted book carries out to the climax.

Romance, too, holds out its own spell. The reader who hastily bought a paperback "Alison's Lover" before setting out on a train journey, would be very disappointed if when she got into the train and settled down to read, she discovered Alison's Lover to be the name of a famous racehorse or sailing boat.

So a title aims to catch and hold the reader's attention and to summarize the theme of the story. A good title therefore should have four qualities: it must be *appealing* or striking; it must also be *true* or exact ... in other words relevant to the story which is about to be unfolded; it should be *slanted* ... that is worded in such a way that it attracts the kind of reader for whom you are writing. If it is an academic piece, therefore, the title will be couched in a different form from an article written for a popular magazine. And finally, as well as being appealing, exact and slanted, a title should usually be *brief*. There isn't room for a title of more than a few words in a newspaper or magazine,

35

though recently long titles are being increasingly used for humorous effect (*A Funny Thing Happened To Me On the Way to the Forum*).

A noun, phrase, question or statement can also form the basis of a title. So can our old friends: WHO, HOW, WHEN, WHAT. Here are some examples of each, taken from work of mine that has been published or broadcast:

NOUN TITLE
A New Pair of Shoes
Fairy Godfather
First Book
PHRASE TITLE
By Candlelight
In Strange Languages
Camping For Fun
QUESTION TITLE
How's The Family?
STATEMENT TITLE
Tom Sends A Valentine
We Shall Have Music
There's Gold Under Your Roof
WHO, WHEN, WHAT, HOW, TITLE
These are all good leads for advice articles: What you Know or Don't Know About . . . ; What to do When. . . . Your Child Gets Measles; How To . . . Make a Rug; Build A Swimming Pool in Your Garden; When. . . . Your Child Starts School.

Choose the structure form that suits you best, or for which the editor shows a preference. Remember that your title should have four qualities: appeal, truth, slant, brevity. To help you achieve a good title, you may like to use one of the following seven aids:

1. *Alliteration:* a group of words beginning with the same sound or letter as in the following piece taken from *The Mikado:*

> To sit in solemn silence in a dull dark dock,
> In a pestilential prison with a lifelong lock
> Awaiting the sensation of a short, sharp shock
> From a cheap and chippy chopper on a big black block.
> (Title example: Prams and Pensions
> Don't Penalize the Pensioner
> Dying Like A Dog)

2. *Allusion* means making a reference (alluding) to a well-known phrase, which might take the form of a pun.
   Title Example: The House That Jill Built
   　　　　　　　Sell Me A Story
   　　　　　　　A Fête Worse Than Death
3. *Repetition:* repeating words or phrases for emphasis
   Title Example: By Thy Light We Shall See Light
   　　　　　　　People Need People
   　　　　　　　A Vote is A Vote is A— (On Elections)
4. *Contrast* means balancing one set of words against another
   Title Example: Saving and Spending
   　　　　　　　For Love Or Money
   　　　　　　　Pigmy versus Giant
5. *Rhythm* is difficult for all but the poets and copy writers to achieve. It means using the stresses and beats of poetry in your title.
   Title Example: The Thunder That Knocked at The Door
   　　　　　　　Angling in Desolate Streams
6. Or you may inject *rhyme* into your title:
   Title Example: New Cook: New Look
   　　　　　　　The Name's To Blame
7. *Humour* is the final and perhaps the best aid to finding a striking or memorable title, but one of the hardest.
   Title Example: Unnatural Feeding
   　　　　　　　Beggar My Neighbour
   　　　　　　　Baby Talk

The above three articles were published as humorous pieces in *Mother and Baby, Punch, Sunday Times*.

Spend an evening or several evenings creating, if you can, different titles for the articles and stories you see in your favourite magazine. Remember the four qualities needed in a title: appeal, exactness or relevance, slant, and brevity. Use any structural form you like: noun, phrase, question, statement, or the HOW, WHEN, WHY, WHAT, type. And if you get stuck, don't forget that there are at least seven aids to help you achieve the aim of catching and holding the elusive reader, and persuading a cynical editor that this is the piece for which he has been waiting all his long life.

CHAPTER 8

LETTERS

INSTANT communication by television, radio and 'phone, causes people to forget how much can be accomplished by a letter. Yet letters have been the beginning of great romances, and they have led people to death. In a famous murder case, 28-year-old Edith Thompson wrote some letters to a 20-year-old clerk, Frederick Bywaters, employed on the P. & O. Liners, who was infatuated by her. One day he came home, met Mrs. Thompson and her husband in an Ilford Street and, in spite of her protests, stabbed the 32-year-old husband to death.

Edith Thompson had not helped with the act, and did not know of it in advance. but the letters which she had written to Bywaters, and which he had unfortunately kept were used to incriminate her in the act of murder. In the letters she had discussed the use of poison and of powdered glass: perhaps in an imaginative way like a crime story, without meaning any real harm to her husband. But the law holds, that when two or more persons co-operate in an attempt at a crime, and in the execution of that crime one of the accomplices kills another person, both the killer and his aide can be charged with murder.

Edith Thompson's letters were construed by the jury as revealing her in the role of an accomplice to the murder. One of the jury is said to have written later to the *Daily Telegraph* that "Mrs. Thompson's letters were her own condemnation". The moral climate of the time proved to be her executioner. In spite of great public outcry, she and Bywaters were both hanged on January 9, 1923.

Not only crimes but memorable romances have stemmed from letters. Consider the extraordinary love story of Robert and Elizabeth Barrett Browning. She was an invalid poet, immured in her room; he, a young energetic man, many years her junior. Having read and been moved by her poems, he wrote to her and managed to get invited to her home ... an accomplishment in itself. From thence the romance blossomed mainly by correspondence until they were finally able to leave her tyrannical father's home, get married and live almost happily ever afterwards in Italy. It sounds too good to be true, yet it happened. Read the letters and see.

Or get those of Frieda von Richthofen to her second husband D. H. Lawrence. The letters reveal not only their emotions but the extra-ordinarily different backgrounds they came from. Lawrence was the clever schoolmaster son of a Nottingham miner, and so well used to the struggle for daily bread that he was stunned by Frieda's inability to turn on the gas tap to boil water when they met in the house she shared with her first husband, a Professor teaching in England.

Read the letters of Florence Nightingale and note her grasp of detail, her administrative brilliance, which had to find an outlet through Parliamentarian friends, for there was even less opportunity then for women to act directly in the political or economic field than there is today.

Read Lady Hamilton's letters, and you will note, happily, that to the furtherance of romance, bad spelling is not an obstacle, and may even have especial charms of its own.

Other famous letter writers worth perusing are Lady Mary Wortley Montagu, Charles Lamb, Horace Walpole, William Cowper and Lord Chesterfield. If you want to read a story told in letter form and can manage three volumes, try *Clarissa* by Richardson, a fascinating old world novel with a charm all its own. There are also the 'shorts' by modern practitioners like Richard Sherman or William Hazlitt Upson. *Simple Arithmetic*, is a good example of a short story in letter form. Written by Virginia Moriconi, it was first published in *Transatlantic Review*, 1963, and reprinted in *The Best American Short Stories, 3*. Observe how cleverly the characters of child, father, mother and stepmother are conveyed with hardly a descriptive line. Note the classic ending, a postscript which simply but convincingly conveys such a wealth of meaning and understanding of a child's world.

For children, there is the perennial *Daddy Long Legs* by Jean Webster, still going strong after twenty-five years in print.

Do not, however, get too carried away with the art of letter writing, or you may become like Lewis Carroll. He kept a register of the letters he wrote beginning when he was twenty-nine years of age. The last item, entered just before his death at sixty-seven, was numbered 98,721. He is not the only prolific letter writer. When Mr. Algernon Ashton died in 1937 at the age of 77, he had had more than 2,000 letters published in the press. The Reverend J. Bacon Phillips of Burgess Hill, could claim a total exceeding 4,000 and so could Mr. B. Simmons, Jun., of Worthing. His first letter was published in a London evening newspaper on August 1, 1903, and the last, just after his death in 1954. An even more prolific letter writer was Mr. Raymond Cantwell with 9,000 published letters to his credit. But even he did not aspire to the length of over 3,000 feet achieved by Miss Terry Finch in a 1969 letter to her boy friend Sergeant Jerry Sullivan.

"Writers should think about the satisfaction they can get from writing letters to editors", says Jim Alkins, a freelance mail order copy writer of Alexandria, Virginia, U.S.A. "My letters have been published in everything from *Newsweek* to the *Washington Post*. Writing letters teaches you to slant your material. It gives you satisfaction and gets your name in important publications."

Lewis Carroll wrote a little book about letter writing with a couple of tips which may be still useful today. He suggested that when answering a letter, it should be read through first, so that the points raised should be specifically answered. He also advised addressing and stamping the envelope before writing the letter, so that the destination is written legibly and without haste. If you are rushed for time, or trying to catch the last post, this can be a useful hint . . . as I have discovered for myself.

But whether you are a prolific or a sporadic letter writer, you will note that all letters can be divided into four types: *appealing*, in which you are asking for something, however subtle your request may be; *placating*, in which you are trying to soothe an irate customer, reader, or trying in the most tactful possible way, to solve somebody's difficulties or to prevent their ire going any further.

The third type of letter is what I call the *denouncing* kind, in which you are complaining or accusing; writing in great dudgeon about the machine that doesn't work, the commodity you have bought that has broken down or proved unsatisfactory; the bad service you got, the bus/train that arrived late or didn't turn up at all.

The final type of letter, and this groups all the rest, is the *stating* kind. A statement doesn't necessarily mean a prosaic recital of facts. It can be a romantic declaration: 'I love you' is as much a statement of fact as is 'Your account is overdrawn'.

Because these letters are all of different types, they have to be phrased in different ways. Your aim is different. If you are making an appeal, for example, you are trying to get some end product or service, to elicit some specific response, whereas when you state a fact you merely draw attention to it.

The most important letter of appeal that anybody is likely to make in a lifetime is the application for a job. At high level, many appointments are made by industrial consultants. Personal contacts are used, but even at high level a letter may serve as the bait to land the required fish into the net.

A good letter lifts an applicant out of the general mass of job-seekers. Putting forward your qualifications and experience in as attractive a light as possible will at least get you up to the hurdle of the first interview. If any qualifications are mentioned in an advertisement for a job, refer to these specific points in your reply. So if an employer wants a short-hand typist with 120 w.p.m. shorthand and 60 w.p.m. typing, show that you have, or soon will be able to reach those speeds. Provide photo-copied references or certificates, and keep your originals for any interviews, and of course you are always leaving your present job for personal advancement—or to transfer to another area—never because you don't like the boss, or the people with whom you are currently working, or the work you are now doing. Such reasons spell 'trouble-maker' to the employer looking for new staff.

Appealing letters want *response* so (save for job applications which tend to be rather stereotyped) they may adopt any style which achieves the required end. As an example, what M.P. could not fail to be moved—and quickly—by this real-life letter with the words, "Dear Sir, This is rather important to me. I am due to be executed on Tuesday. . . ."?

In stories and feature articles, a writer tries to make arresting openings and satisfying conclusions. In a letter it is the *tone* which is most important. By tone is meant language or style fitting to the occasion. If you have no idea how to achieve the correct tone, try writing two letters, one to the Queen or member of the Royal household asking if she/he would ceremonially open a new road/hospital/school, in the borough, and another to a member of your school swimming/tennis/football club, telling him/her that the next match has been cancelled. This exercise tells you something about *tone*. It is the same as the feature writer's slanting for a reader.

The tone in a job application should be formal . . . that is not chatty or breezy but courteous and dignified. Don't grovel: the employer may need you even more than you need him. And none of the six basic points of the letter should be forgotten:

1. The address of the sender in the right hand top corner.
2. The date beneath it.
3. The address and title of the recipient lower down on the left hand side.
4. The salutation or form of address below, e.g. Dear Sir (or Dear Mrs. Smith.) Charles Lamb is said to have addressed a firm, Bensusan and Co. as Dear Sir and Madam, but do not imitate him, at least in this respect.
5. The text or body of the letter.
6. The conclusion: Yours faithfully: or Yours truly, or whatever is appropriate.

In business letters, a seventh point may be necessary, namely, a heading to the letter, after Dear Sir, and before the main body of the letter begins.

The tone or style of the letter will be changed by points 4 the salutation, 5 the text, and 6 the conclusion. If, for example, you begin your letter My Lord Bishop, you won't end it "With lots of love from Your Rector." If you begin it "My Dearest Beloved" you won't end it "Yours faithfully". This is perhaps why Victor Hugo's letter to his publisher consisting of the one symbol '?' received the reply '!', a succinct and fitting criticism to a query about Hugo's novel, *Les Misérables*.

After the letter of appeal comes the *denouncing* letter. In this you are complaining. Remember the A.B.C. of all business letters, Accuracy, Brevity, Courtesy. In making the complaint give particulars of the faulty equipment, its number, if any, when and where purchased; or the time when a service should have been given and wasn't, and dates.

Remember a good rule of the negotiating table: always offer a way out. Leave room for compromise or amends. To denounce or complain without giving an opportunity for recompense or apology is very short-sighted. A good denouncing letter should induce the response that you most want.

A *placating* letter is one which firms have to write so often that in many large concerns, there is a department specifically for customers' complaints, and replies to them. Before any placating letters are written, justice demands that there should be some investigation into the truth of the complaints. This may not be within your province, and will in any case take time, so a card saying that "Your letter of . . . regarding . . . is receiving attention," or even more briefly "Your letter is receiving attention", will take a bit of the pressure off for a week or two at least. Not to acknowledge a denouncing letter is asking for yet more trouble. The correspondent may give up. On the other hand you risk his/her ire growing to such dimensions that it can spark off a major publicity campaign or even a question in Parliament.

If it is decided to give some recompense for bad service/commodities/ repairs, or to adjust a timetable, the tone of your letter will be fairly unimportant. The person who receives your letter is going to be less interested in the wording than the recompense, etc., offered. But if it has been decided that the customer's complaint is an unjust one or has no foundation, and you have the job of writing a 'brush-off' letter, phrase your reply in as courteous and as tactful a way as you can.

In one office in which I was employed, instead of writing Dear Mrs. So and So to customers complaining about their washing and other machines, and the service or lack of service received, the letters always began My Dear Mrs. So and So. I didn't notice that this had any more soothing effect on Dear Mrs. So and So but it was an effort in the right direction.

Stating letters can be subdivided into numerous different kinds: letters written to the press, informative letters, letters which are really reports. The best method of grouping *stating* letters, however, is into formal ones used mostly for business and those which are more personal. For business letters, say what you have to say, accurately, briefly, courteously. (A.B.C.)

Dear Sir,

As your account was overdrawn on the 1st March by £50, your annual standing order for £100 to the Magnificat Insurance Company could not be paid. Please remit the necessary funds as soon as possible.

Yours faithfully . . .

Private letters are formally worded when this is appropriate as, for example, when answering a formal invitation: Mr. and Mrs. Hawkins thank the Principal for the invitation to the Prizegiving and are very glad to accept. Similarly to a formal wedding invitation or to a reception. If, however, you are asked by your good friend Dave to an All Night Rave Up (or similar) to celebrate a coming of age or any other informal celebration, sincerity is the keynote: You'd love to come.

A woman's magazine editor who publishes a letter column with small prizes offered every month, once gave the following order of importance for letters received:

Firstly, they had to be authentic . . . that is genuine. They had to be sincere, provocative, original, humorous, of human interest, brief and topical. She also recommended that the letters be legible.

Another type of letter, which can come into any of the four groups so far outlined, is one that is written for reward: for publication with payment. The best way of tackling these is to keep an indexed notebook especially for letter ideas. Enter any ideas, sayings, observations, topicalities that crop up into the appropriate alphabetical heading. Make a list of the magazines and newspapers which publish and pay for letters.

Against each magazine or newspaper title, put down the slant the editor prefers, judging at least from the pieces he publishes. Notice how long the pieces are, whether they are in the first or third person; whether he prefers children's sayings, recipes, travel tips, or any other observations you can deduce about the editor's preferences. Slanting your letters to suit him is one of the secrets of successful letter writing and selling.

Lastly, there are letters written for publication without reward. This is a most useful form of apprenticeship for any writer. He can say exactly what he thinks without fear or favour. Notice any amendments or deletions the editor may make. They show the writer what is most acceptable, the type of material the editor wants, and how he likes it worded. For a young writer hoping one day to get published *and* be paid for it, there is no more valuable lesson than that.

CHAPTER 9

WRITE HIGH, AIM LOW

In one of Henry James's books there is a passage describing Milan Cathedral seen from above: the gargoyles, the soaring spires, the decorated stonework. These embellishments are quite invisible from below, yet they were added to make a beautiful whole. Why, the author asks, and fortunately gives us the answer.

When the cathedral was built, the worker was activated by two ideas: joy in craft for its own sake and as his own personal offering to God. His finished product had to be as perfect as he could devise: it reflected his skill as a craftsman, and it was a tribute to his Creator. Whether another man could see the work or not was of no consequence. God could.

The desire for perfection on such a scale is not so evident today. People are often very skilled in manual crafts, as the Do-It-Yourself movement shows. Many workers spend leisure time beautifying their homes and gardens and get from this pursuit a sense of achievement. By contrast, their daily work does not give them this feeling. Packaging, machining, doing monotonous clerical or factory work under conditions of noise, heat, ugliness, speed or stress ... which is the lot of many millions ... do not engender great enthusiasm, particularly if the end product is neither seen nor known.

And the motive of working for the greater glory of God, or to bear witness, today inspires only the most saintly or selfless among us.

But the artist (like the man or woman who dedicates his life for the love of God to the betterment of his fellow man), is an exception. No matter what his art form may be, he strives, like the monks and guildsmen of old, for perfection.

This is not because he gets more satisfaction from the completion of work which he feels to be worthwhile than from turning out what he knows in his heart to be rubbish, for this first satisfaction may not last

45

or indeed may never come. His work may not be acknowledged to be good, a lack of recognition which may cause him such misery or privation that he may even take his own life. He has never learnt to say, with Fontaine, "There is this consolation in the work which one undertakes for God, that He asks of us the work itself, not its success."

His inspiration has to be the unknown reader, the unseen viewer of today or tomorrow. Somewhere, at some time, the work on which the writer is now engaged, will be read. Somewhere, at some time, it is going to make an impression on an unknown reader. The writer may never meet this reader on whom his words will make such an impact, so he must choose them well. In this one person's mind they may live for ever.

It is often alleged that writers are motivated only by money. But if the reward for work is in part financial, a writer must judge his success at least in part by the payment he receives. When people buy his books or his stories, he knows the output on which he has laboured, has succeeded, for it has found readers. Johnson's saying "only a fool writes for anything but money" is but half true. The rewards for successful writing are in (i) the act of creation (ii) being published and (iii) being paid.

The beginner to writing is in a very privileged position. He can strive for excellence, risking nothing, and with the chance of gaining everything: publication, payment, prestige, response. He needs the same spirit of dedication as the monk-workers of old, even if he lacks their motivation. This does not mean that he has to turn out only spiritually uplifting passages: it means he must produce the best of which he is capable in his own field.

Tragedy is often regarded as a higher literary form than comedy, perhaps because unfulfilled promise, which tragedy is, has more piquancy for the reader. It emphasizes the ephemeral quality of life, the shortness of our span in the eternal universe. Because of this stress on our transitory existence, tragedy moves us more deeply then comedy.

But being an entertainer or giving people enjoyment, interest and information is every bit as worthwhile a task as is the writing of a tragedy or other literary masterpiece. It improves the quality of life. It extends a man's vision. So a writer who gives his best to his own niche, however small, must believe in his work. Because it may alter the course of a man's life, it is as important as the 'greatest' novel.

The writer must produce work which he has fashioned as perfectly as he knows how, aim as high in his work as the builders of Gothic churches. They knew that only the immortal Creator could see the whole of the vision they had fashioned in His name and to His glory. The writer, is working for an equally invisible but mortal human Being who deserves respect and reverence, too.

Rejection can, however, wither the tender buds of creativity, so the beginning writer must aim low for his first sales. A cheque for a well-written piece in the Rabbit Lovers Diary, or the Carpet Weavers News gives him more stimulus than the friendliest rejection slip from a mass circulation daily or prestige weekly.

The fact that a writer tries to produce a perfect piece does not unfortunately make it acceptable to an editor or publisher. The writer may have gone so wrong that the work is quite unpublishable.

The most common fault that beginners make in features is to choose the wrong subject. The piece may have narrative appeal, provocative ideas, but it is formless: a collection of points adding up to a big nothing. The writer has taken a subject and failed to hold it together, to give it a conclusion. The remedy for this defect is to work from a point of view, and to hold on to this throughout the article. It will give a meaning and cohesion to the work.

The second fault is often the lack of a market. More will be said on this in Part Two: Markets and Marketing. But for the moment always ask yourself before beginning a piece and alas when you have finished, Who cares? Who is interested in this piece? The answer gives your market. The more people who care or can be made to care, the bigger your market. Instead of going for universal or mass appeal, you can sometimes emphasize uniqueness ... the only one of its kind in the world, the strangest romance, the perfect crime. This element of uniqueness attracts as large a number of readers as the article with an obvious mass appeal.

There are a miniscule number of soldiers who have married Presidents' daughters, or Cinderellas who have married Presidents' sons; these events do not happen every day, but it is their very uniqueness which makes them a universal draw. So check whether your subject has a universal appeal. If not, try slanting it to be unique.

The third fault is similar to the second: namely wrong market. As an illustration, imagine you have written a very interesting and provocative article on diabetes with plenty of incidents and facts and even a potted life story of Banting and the discovery of insulin, thrown in. You then send the piece to the Spastics Recorder. Obviously a magazine for Spastics is going to be interested mainly in articles which have a relevance for them. You must find a different market.

Take a universally appealing subject: travel. If you are writing about a very expensive kind of holiday with air travel to South Africa from England and a safari tour thrown in: or crossing the States with luxury hotels all along the route: or even a tour to Australia or Japan: this kind of expensive holiday is not going to be within the compass of an indigent pensioners' magazine. Check therefore whether your good subject has gone to the wrong market. Students, pensioners and others on low incomes want concrete facts about the cheapest eating houses, hostels, routes, and where to find lifts.

To learn the art of marketing, try to write a travel article geared to the needs of different kinds of magazine readers: one for impecunious gentlefolk, one for young married couples with small children, and lastly for the very rich. This exercise will emphasize how very important it is to gear your subject to a market. Perhaps the most common fault of all beginners is to write in a vacuum: to create a story or feature first, and then to think of a market. In today's competitive world, the market should be at least tentatively thought of first, and the writing then geared to meet that need.

Never, never, just take the name of a magazine or newspaper from *The Writers' and Artists' Year Book* and write for it according to the specifications listed. If you are a gifted writer or have had many credits to your name, you may possibly be lucky. Usually it will be a waste of time and effort. Beginners should always get a copy of a magazine before attempting to write for it. Half a dozen issues will give you the 'feel' of the magazine, the type of feature or story published and increase your chances of getting acceptances instead of rejections.

The fourth most common mistake of beginners is no style. This is such a generalized criticism, and so hard to correct. How does one achieve style? What is it? Style is the imprint of the artist; the trade mark he gives to his work so that it is immediately recognizable.

It is impossible to pick up one of Hemingway's or Graham Greene's books without recognizing the hand that wrote it. Similarly with poetry: the almost colloquial simplicity of Robert Frost, the complexity and depth of Auden, the subject matter of Betjeman. In painting, too, with its subject, colour, brushwork; in music and sculpture, the great artist always imprints his own style on the material with which he works.

How then can a beginner learn to improve or develop his style? All I can say here is that a man becomes what he loves. If a writer immerses himself in works that have stood the test of time, something of their greatness will rub off on to him.

Analyse wherein lies the attraction of an artist. Get to know more of his work, to be able to recognize it and sometimes even to imitate it. Don't strive for effect. Read constantly: books for entertainment and light relief as well as the classics. To get the most succinct and perceptive summing up of what a writer's attitude to his craft should be, read W. H. Auden's poem, *The Novelist*.

Closely allied to the question of style is the writing that seems dull or boring. Liven it up with a few quotes. Give a few illustrations and examples. Try a new way of looking at your theme. In stories, use active verbs to get pace and movement. View the piece from a different angle and change a story from third to first person to see whether the effect is more vivid and lively.

After poor style, the next fault and cause of possible rejections is lack of facts. 'Think' pieces (opinions) are wanted only if they have such great passion that they can move people, or if they come from writers famous in their own right. Otherwise almost all feature articles need facts: statistics, information, prices and other details to support the theme. If you find this difficult to do, a table is a useful help for a beginner. Draw a grid and put your details into that, and your ideas into the main body of your text. See the table below taken from the author's article on 'Camping' published in *She* magazine.

Lastly, there is the question of timing. This applies not only to features but to short stories and novels. Some novels have become best sellers because they came out at just the right time. Good anticipation is one way of being successful with timing. Professional authors often have biographies of people written awaiting the death of their subject to increase the sales potential—much in the manner of newspapers who keep obituaries of famous personages to print when they die.

You will need	Where obtainable	Cost

Tent
 	
Beds
(*a*) lilos or air beds
(*b*) camp beds
 	
Sleeping bags
	To buy: from camping stockists:
	Casey's, 66 Stapleton Road, Bristol, 5
	Marble Arch Stores, 276/302
	Camberwell Road, London, S.E.5
	Benjamin Edgington, 144/146
	    Shaftesbury Avenue, London,
	    W.C.2 (also hire out everything
	    featured in their brochure)
	To hire: John Edgington, 50/52
	    Neate Street, London, S.E.5
	Continental Camping Hire Services
	    Ltd., 9 High Street, Penge
	    London, S.E.20
		To buy:
		(1) Tents: *Frame* from
		    £25 *Igloo or Poleless*
		    from £20 *Ridge*
		    around £6 upwards
		(2) Beds: *Lilos* from 30/-
		    Camp beds from
		    about £2
		(3) Sleeping bags:
		    Single from £2
		    Double from £5
		    (Hire costs vary)

Cookers
(*a*) Primus
(*b*) Bottled Gas
(*c*) Expendable
    Cartridge
    appliances
	(*a*) Camping equipment stores
	(*b*) Sports Continentale, 5/7 Totten-
	    ham Street, London, W.1; and
	    other stockists. (There are stockists
	    throughout Europe)
	(*c*) As under (*a*)
		(*a*) About £2
		(*b*) Various prices:
		    a 4 lb. cylinder
		    would cost about
		    £3–£4 (refills 10/-
		    15/-)
		(*c*) Bleuet Stove about
		    38/-, cartridges 3/6

Cooking equipment	Millet's; Girl Guide Headquarters	Various prices
Folding table four stools	All stockists	Wooden at about £2/10/- more for lightweight

**Camping club
    membership**
	Camping Club of Gt. Britain,
	    11 Lower Grosvenor Place,
	    London, S.W.1
		Entrance fee 10/-
		Annual Sub: 35/- for the
		    first year, then 25/-
		Additional Family mem-
		    bership 2/6 each

**Year book with
    list of camp
    sites**
	From above address on payment of
	    membership fee
		Fees at listed sites in
		    Britain: around 2/-
		    per person per night

List of foreign camp sites	2/- post free from the Camping Club	

Books
*Enjoy Camping
Holidays* by Alan
Ryalls; Gollancz
*Caravan and Camping
Sites and Farmhouse
Accommodation in
Britain*
The Sites Handbook
 	
Camping Abroad by
A. G. E. Beanland
*Expedition Everyman
1964* by S. B.
Hough; Hodder
and Stoughton
	All booksellers
	
	British Travel and Holidays
	    Association, 64 St. James's Street,
	    London, S.W.1
	
	H. G. Walters (Publishers) Ltd.,
	    Market Square, Narberth, Pembs.
	Percival Marshall, 19/20 Noel Street,
	    London, W.1
	All booksellers
		10/6
		
		3/6
		
		2/6
		
		5/-
		3/6

Feature articles and stories with a topical theme should always be submitted to monthly magazines six months before publication date. They have to be as forward looking as fashion in clothes. The following story may astonish some readers but I can vouch for its accuracy. I once submitted a piece to *The Guardian* called, 'Dying Like a Dog'. It was I thought, (but naturally) an excellent piece and so ideally suited to *The Guardian* I could not think of a better market. I sent it out on March 30, and it came back in days with a rejection slip. I put the piece dejectedly away.

Three and a half years later, going through some of my old manuscripts, I came across the piece again, and still could not understand why it had been rejected. I did something I have never done before or since: sent it back to the same market. The date of submission was October 7, and it was published on November 7. The article described poverty, and November–December are the months when people think about Christmas and their hearts respond more easily to appeals. So my piece got in. This is the best story on the importance of timing that I can give you.

Novels may similarly fail because they are too early or too late, or do brilliantly because they come out at a good moment. It was difficult to get scenes portraying sexual permissiveness fifty years ago. It may be equally hard to get themes of fidelity or chastity published today. What is barely acceptable in one generation is 'old hat' in another.

In a children's novel, *The Mystery of The Blue Tomatoes*, which I wrote in 1958, I introduced what was then the taboo of 'foreigners': Japanese. I did this deliberately to show that there were good and bad foreigners, white or yellow, just as there were good and bad natives. I introduced, too, a working class family in a New Town, when the general tone of children's books of the fifties was middle class, with ponies, boarding schools, absent parents and ballet as the pet subjects. Strangely, perhaps, it was accepted on the strength of the opening three chapters at its first submission, probably because an ex-children's librarian was at that time children's book editor.

The book was recommended in the *Schoolgirls' Diary* as one of the best books of the year, a verdict with which I (naturally) agreed. But it got hardly any publicity, no national reviews, and sales just reached 5,000. I think it was too early. Parents and teachers then bought children's books and they wanted middle class language, background and characters. Some years later 'realism' pervaded the children's book market, and secondary modern school characters became all the rage.

So if you have looked at all the possible points where you may have gone wrong: subject, market, style, lack of facts, dullness and found these in order, give another look at your timing. It may be you are too early or what is far worse and far more common . . . too late.

And here finally are some questions to test the article that comes back with a rejection slip.

1. Has my article *point*? Can I sum up its theme in a sentence?
2. Is it *relevant*? Have I inserted unnecessary details or wandered from my theme?
3. Does my piece entertain, inform, inspire?
4. Is it *new* or a rehash of old material?
5. Is it related to *people* or written in abstract terms which will move nobody?
6. What about style? Is the piece dull, written at the level of my readers, above or below them? Is my vocabulary adequate or exciting?
7. What about the *lead*? Does it give my most interesting piece of information or narration? Does it make the reader want to read on?
8. Do I make my statistics clear, or does the reader have to translate them? Are my facts and figures given in terms which the reader can immediately understand?
9. What about my ending? Does it sum up the theme of the piece? Does it leave the reader with a glow of satisfaction, or does it fizzle out like a damp squib?
10. Is my MS. well typed? Is the spelling accurate (check with a dictionary.) Does it look *interesting* or are there long, heavy paragraphs unenlivened by quotes, similes, or dialogue?
11. Did I send it out in time?

If you can answer 'Yes' to all these questions, then it is not you but the editor who is at fault. Your piece deserves to be sent to somebody a bit more perspicacious.

But if you cannot answer 'Yes' to all these questions, there is only one remedy, REWRITE!

Part Two

MARKETS AND MARKETING

CHAPTER 10

BUSINESS COMMUNICATION

ALTHOUGH business communication, is not usually thought of as a form of creative writing, its impact on the reader (and sometimes on the writer) can be even more important than a best selling novel. The writer, by memo., report, or article in a house journal, reveals his ability to write simply, logically and persuasively, or his capacity for riling readers and communicating misleading information.

The reader is influenced in his actions by the information and instructions he receives. When, as in a Trade Union group, there are several thousand to a million readers, the effects can be momentous. Think of all the go-slow (work-to-rule) strikes that have been made possible by keeping to the letter of highly detailed operating and instruction manuals.

Business communication is therefore a very important test of writing skills. It includes the compilation and dissemination of memos., minutes, reports, instruction manuals as well as articles for house journals. And this is not all. Films, visual aids, broadcasting, closed circuit television are also used for communication in business (and in education.) Although such aids make a bigger immediate impact on a larger number of people, their message is more short lived. The written word endures, can be looked up and referred to, again and again. How then can success be achieved in this immense field?

The first requirement of all communication is that it should be intelligible between sender and receiver. That outsiders cannot understand is of no consequence (and from the viewpoint of industrial espionage may be an advantage!). To ensure that his communication is intelligible the sender of information must have an understanding of the subject matter, the medium he is using to convey it, and of the audience receiving it . . . or simply: what, how and who. If an instructor training young workers by means of a film, puts the film in backwards, or discovers he is showing 'How to be a Model' to his trainee chefs instead of 'How to Run a Motel', which he had ordered, the trainees are likely to have an uproarious time. But entertainment was not the object of the exercise. The instructor has failed in his task of communicating the right information. He was not in command of the medium he was using to convey information.

The second requirement of business communication is that it should be accurate and, so far as is possible, brief.

As an aid to the first requirement of intelligibility, here are some definitions:

A memo.—short for memorandum—is a brief report prepared on the writer's own initiative for circulation to management, or to a particular person or department within the firm.

First comes the name of the person, department or group to whom the information is addressed, thus: *TO ALL STAFF.*

The communication then follows. It is headed with a summary of the contents: *HOLIDAY ARRANGEMENTS, 1980*

Under the title or summary heading, should come the memo. itself, which is an expansion of the idea(s) embodied in the heading, thus:

In order that holiday arrangements can be completed as soon as possible, all staff are requested to submit their requirements before February 28, 1980.

The memo. should give the name and rank of the person issuing it, and the date:

J. F. HAGEDORN,
Branch Manager: 1:12:1979

A lengthy document will not always be read to the end, particularly if it is pinned up in a busy department of the works, such as the canteen, where single-file readers are unlikely. Memos. for factory and shop floor should therefore always be short.

Minutes are a record of the business transacted at a meeting and of the decisions reached. A Secretary is usually responsible for taking a record of the views expressed at a meeting and writing it up later concisely and accurately. The completed 'minutes', as they are then known, are usually read at the next meeting, unless they have previously been circulated to members.

If the company present agree that the minutes as read are an accurate record of the proceedings, the Chairman signs them as such. If they are not accepted as accurate, the Chairman corrects the minute and initials it. Alternatively, and preferably, he may refer to the incorrect minute when he signs, thus. 'The minutes of the meeting on . . . were confirmed and signed by the Chairman, subject to the inclusion of the name of Mrs. J. Hagedorn in the list of members appointed as a special sub-committee to consider the possibility of introducing wages and pensions for wives employed wholly at home.'

After the Chairman has signed the minutes, no alteration is permissible without a resolution being passed to that effect.

Because the aim of the minutes is to record all business transactions and views expressed, sufficient information should be included to make the record useful for reference purposes (such as contract specifications, proposed sites, or names of people appointed to committees).

Help in the writing of minutes may be obtained from the standing orders which govern minute taking. It may be found, for example, that only the numbers for and against each resolution must be given, or, alternatively, only the name of the proposer and seconder for the resolution. Where no regulations govern procedure, the Minutes Secretary can use his or her own discretion as to how much to leave in or out. He should remember always, however, that the concise recording of business discussed, views expressed and decisions taken, is the aim in taking minutes.

Reports differ from memos. in (i) length and (ii) origin. They are always longer. Some, such as the Radcliffe Report, Crowther Report or the Milner Holland Report, to name but a few well-known ones, run into hundreds of pages. Furthermore they are written not on the initiative of a particular writer in a particular department, but as the result of a request by a body of interested people; or by a superior in a department or at head office.

Unlike a memo., which gives out information or instructions to be acted upon, a report investigates a problem in depth, giving recommendations only for its solution. The recommendations can be ignored. They have no legal or administrative force. If a member of the group issuing a report dissents strongly from the majority decision, he records his dissent in an appendix.

The title of the report indicates the problem being investigated: Railway Policy; Fuel Policy. When the report achieves widespread publicity, the title generally becomes obscured in favour of the Chairman's name, thus the Radcliffe Report (An Enquiry into the Workings of the Monetary System), The Milner Holland Report (A Report into Rented Accommodation in London), or the Parker Morris Report (Homes for the Future).

The first paragraph should deal with the aim of the report. Many reports fail to attract readers because they have too long a lead-in (introduction). They give lots of facts about the topic under discussion, but take the reader away from the main objective, namely the topic the report is investigating, and why.

Facts about the present situation come next. Possible solutions to the problem are then suggested by the members of the committee issuing the report, together with the advantages and disadvantages (if any). An appendix can be added, so that supplementary information will not obscure the clarity of the main body of the report.

Instruction Manuals are basically an extension of the 'How To . . .' article. The technique is to break down the instructions into a sequence of simple steps or operations. The danger in writing 'How To' articles is of assuming the reader to be a moron . . . but is better that than, for example, a patient using a medicament with wrapping because the instructions have neglected to say 1. Remove wrapping.

Finally, House Journals and Works Magazines are other forms of business communication. They circulate within an industry composed of a number of different departments or buildings. The editor may be a paid employee whose job is to produce the magazine within a scheduled budget. If he gets his writers cheaply or his production costs down, in effect he gets a personal bonus. He has more freedom than the other type of editor, also a paid employee, who produces a magazine, the costs of which are borne by another department.

A third form of house journal is one produced and edited by an outside public relations or advertising firm for a negotiated fee.

The works magazine proper gives personal news items of staff; contributions made by various parts of the factory or works to the smooth running of the organization, details of people and operations at work in various departments, and any new management ideas for public dissemination, e.g. pilfering on unattended sites and ideas to reduce these thefts. If the aim of the magazine is to increase the flow of ideas in the industry and to improve labour relations, it is distributed to the staff without charge. Freelance work is welcomed from contributors within the works, provided it is of general interest and fits in with the aims of the magazine. It is sometimes paid for, but there is little or no opportunity for unsolicited contributions from outsiders.

Works magazines on sale to the general public are usually referred to as house journals. They exist not only to improve labour relations, but to help improve the image of the company or industry and to sweeten consumer relations. Particulars of most house journals can be found in *Willings Press Guide* or the *Newspaper Press Directory*, both available in public libraries.

Many writers can find a useful paying niche in these magazines. The payment depends on the standard of the publication, the amount of money allocated by the company for its production and of course on the quality of work submitted by the writer. If you assume a rate comparable to the trade or professional magazine, you won't go far wrong.

CHAPTER 11

ESSAY-TYPE EXAMINATIONS

Answering essay-type examinations is a form of writing for prestige. Passing the examination gives the successful candidate a piece of prestige paper which can cushion his days for the rest of his life.

It doesn't matter whether you disagree with a system by which a person's worth to society or his entry into a certain profession depends not on his intrinsic merit and sometimes not even on his knowledge, but on his ability to write the correct answers to certain questions posed in a certain form in a certain year.

You may find it intolerable that in order to be regarded as fit to teach and to get the wages of a 'qualified' teacher instead of the derisory rate of an 'unqualified' one, if so lowly a specimen is allowed to teach at all, you must spend one, two or three years on irrelevant and outdated study. You may declaim that such study is set by people who have spent little time at close quarters with young children or in the hurly-burly of a large comprehensive school, and that the course ends with written tests which can never really prove how 'qualified' a person is to teach.

No matter. The system is there. Though it may be altered, adapted, worsened or even scrapped in the long term, some type of sieve will still have to be devised to separate the 'successful' from the 'rest'. Meanwhile, if you wish to pass into the hallowed shrine reserved for those legally allowed to practise medicine, accountancy, banking; to teach in state schools or plead in court, you must *correctly* answer the appropriate examination questions.

Now in order to pass any examination, two requirements are necessary (a) knowledge of the subject matter and (b) ability to communicate that knowledge to the examiner in the form he wants it.

The subject matter may be wide and fairly shallow as at 'O' level, or narrow and specific but of much greater depth as in degree type examinations.

The regulations and syllabus lay down the subject matter. And there is no getting away from the fact that some part of it at least must be mastered. Notice that we say some part, for herein lies the examinees' salvation. An intelligent perusal of past question papers shows that certain topics constantly recur. To get maximum pass marks in the minimum time, a study in depth of a few favourite topics (which is not education, but examination technique), is likely to give the student higher marks than he will get by trying to encompass everything anybody has ever written about the set syllabus.

As an example, let us take not a subject such as History or Literature which commends itself to the essay writer, but a technical one: Monetary Theory and Practice of the Banking Diploma Examinations. The Syllabus covers Money, Monetary Systems, International Monetary Regulations and British Public Finance. An analysis of past question papers show that seven main topics constantly recur, though phrased in different ways. The topics are Money, Banking, Balance of Payments, Interest Rates, External Matters, Budget (Govt. and Taxation), Money Market with the Bank of England, and a group covering a variety of questions which can be listed under Sundries.

Here is an analysis to cover the questions set from April 1965 to April 1967.

	Apr. 65	Sept. 65	Apr. 66	Sept. 66	Apr. 67
MONEY	Supply and Demand	As a Com-modity	Money Claims	Demand for Money	Monetary Policy
BANKING	Assets of Banks	Central and Com-mercial Banks	Deposits	Deposits	Assets
BALANCE OF PAYMENTS	Current Account	Balance of Payments	Devalu-ation	Terms of Trade	How Balanced
INTEREST RATES	Long Term	Long Term	Gold	Money Supply	Short Term

	Apr. 65	Sept. 65	Apr. 66	Sept. 66	Apr. 67
BUDGET	Monetary Measures	Budget	Taxation	Budget	Budget
MONEY MARKET	Bank Rate	Funding Policy	Credit Control	Money Market	Interest Rates
SUNDRIES	National Debt	Quantity Theory	U.S. Banks	Euro-markets	IBDR

Four questions have to be attempted out of eight. When study time is limited, concentrate on five topics. Exclude (i) Sundries ... too varied; (ii) External Matters ... too diverse; (iii) Interest Rates ... can go in with Money. This leaves the following topics for study: Money, Banking, Balance of Payments, Budget, and the Money Market.

Within four of these topics you can get down to basic key words, e.g. Budget (key words: taxation: aims and means; elasticity of demand), Banking (assets, deposits and control of credit), Money (supply and demand; cf. other commodities) Balance of Payments (currency or capital flows and other money movements; devaluation; terms of trade.) This technique of learning by topics is only a form of writing to a given market. The subject matter, or theme, is laid down. You merely slant it to suit the requirements of your reader (examiner).

The question papers of any other examination can be analysed in the same way. The Corporation of Secretaries tested over several years, the following topics: Business Enterprise, Monopoly, Taxation, Monetary Policy, Prices, International Trade; there was slightly less emphasis on location of industry, wages and population problems.

Using this method of studying the pattern of past questions and concentrating on a limited number of topics, I once gave a young lad six one-hourly lessons in Economics, spread over six weeks. He passed 'A' level not with very great distinction (Grade C), but without any previous knowledge of the subject at all, even at 'O' level. He was nineteen had attempted three and got one 'A' level previously. His aim in taking

Economics was quite utilitarian: he wanted to work for a year in industry to earn some cash, but at the same time to get another 'A' level to qualify for University entrance.

I persuaded him that he could pass any 'A' level essay-type examination after six hours private coaching by the method of study of topics and past questions and suggested he took Economics. It seemed more suitable for him than any of the 'O' level subjects which he had already passed or the 'A's' which he had already attempted and failed.

But do not underestimate the difficulty of acquiring knowledge of the subject matter if you have to study it on your own and have no liking for or aptitude in it at all. Yet somehow this hurdle must be passed either because it is a preliminary to getting a particular qualification or into a desired profession. Concentration on the syllabus to determine from past questions which topics are likely to be raised is merely one solution.

Another is somehow to raise an enthusiasm for the subject which gives difficulty. This is easier said than done. But assume for example, that in English Literature the set books to be studied have been written by what appears to be the dullest lot of authors who ever wielded a pen like a pick-axe.

Take heart. In a Report on the Examining of English Literature comes the following definition of Literature: "writing of such quality that it invites and rewards repeated careful readings". To the student's blinkered eyeballs, the invitation clement appears to be so heavily disguised as to be more of a repellant. Press on, however, and the rewards will truly come as the following example may show.

I was once rung up by a local authority to take, at very short notice, an evening class group who wanted to study English Literature at 'O' level. The students were between 16 and 60. Most of them had failed their exams at school: the rest had never taken any.

One of the set books was Shakespeare's *Twelfth Night*. I had not seen a Shakespeare play since my schooldays many years previously. The thought of even having to look through a play was quite distasteful. Shakespeare! There were so many pleasanter ways of spending time. But having agreed to take the class, it was now imperative to brush up my reading.

Somewhere in the house were *The Complete Works* ... a long-ago prize for First-Year Shorthand. If it had ever been read, it had certainly been long forgotten. Now I began in truly barbarian fashion to read

E

65

through a bit of a Shakespeare play every day over my lunch: at first with fortitude, and then gradually with admiration. By the time the class started I was in a state of infectious enthusiasm.

One of the younger students became an amateur poet, keen as mustard. When he failed to turn up for several weeks we wondered what had happened to him. He returned one evening his leg in plaster. Reading the set book, he had become so taken up with it that he crossed the road into the college without looking up, was hit by a passing motorist and broke a leg. That was his story and he had his plaster to prove it. The local paper published some of his poems afterwards so he obviously possessed a creative imagination in spite of having failed his English exams at school. We got a 100 per cent pass rate in that class and it was one of the most enjoyable of the many enjoyable classes I have taught. Enthusiasm for the subject, however engineered, whether by the necessity of having to teach it, or by group therapy, is more than half way to its mastery.

Another solution is to forget that the shortest distance between two points (you and your aim of passing an examination) is a straight line. Read round the subject. As an example, in English Literature, pick up any good author you personally enjoy. Exhaust his books, or yourself until you feel ready and indeed, eager, to try something else. In this way your ear will become attuned to a feeling for words, an appreciation of different styles and even a passion for books. This will help not only to upgrade your English but any other essay type examinations.

Link subjects if possible. Studying Economic History of the 19th century with English Literature or British Constitution of the same period, gives far better results than would be got from the same utilization of study hours spread over disparate subjects with no link in time, place or theme.

Another method is to tackle the subject, which has to be mastered, indirectly. If your set book is Conrad's *The Rover*, this may seem as sparkling as a stagnant pond compared with a gripping thriller or piece of science fiction. Try, then one of Conrad's other books: *Lord Jim Almayer's Folly*, *Youth*, or his short stories, to get an idea of his style: the waves of description including even the purple passages; the rhythmic cadences; his wonderful ear for the spoken word so that we get the device of Marlow as the narrator in *Lord Jim*; Conrad's philosophy: the isolation of the individual by fate, guilt, chance, a favourite theme for many authors . . . but don't follow up this idea too extensively or you will go right off course.

Read about the author himself. This can be a delicious time-wasting exercise or it can give you some idea of the obstacles he had to overcome to produce his work and make you, as a reader, more sympathetic towards it. Could you, for example, at the age of twenty, begin learning another language, as Conrad did, to such good effect that you obtained a master mariner's certificate and wrote books in that language acknowledged to be literary masterpieces?

Similarly with other subjects. Reading about the self-educated George Boole, later Professor at Queen's College, Cork, will give you a greater appreciation of algebra; or about great men in mathematics, in physics, or chemistry—a better idea of their contribution to the sciences. Many of these innovators have fascinating facets to their characters and were brilliant in other fields besides their own. Reading their life stories can give you an enthusiasm for the subject which inspired and motivated them and which so far has failed to stir you at all. But always remember your objective: acquiring knowledge of the set subject, not of the fascinating bypaths round it.

Gaining the required knowledge, then, is one part of examination technique; the other is of communicating it, and here choice of question (or at thesis level, subject title) is of almost paramount importance. As a marker of Higher National Diplomas and other professional examinations, I have seen more people fail because they chose the wrong question or answered ones they wished had been set, than for any other reason save inadequate preparation and inadequate ability. About the latter there is not much that can be done. We can't all run a four-minute mile: we may have to settle for some different form of satisfaction or achievement. Our talents, such as they are, may be in other fields. But a determination to succeed often overcomes natural disabilities.

Before the examination, have a couple of practice runs to get an idea of the time factor. Divide up the time allowed between the number of questions to be done, so that you do not spread yourself too freely and for too long on one question. *Allow 15 minutes for revision.*

When you get into the examination room and are given the question paper, tick off all the questions about which you can write something. Number them in the order of difficulty they present to you. Before committing your pen to paper make a rough list of the points you are going to cover in your answer.

It sometimes happens that a question which appears very easy at first glance turns out, during a pre-trial run of making rough points, to be very difficult to answer. This is particularly true of those questions asking for comparisons (of advantages, disadvantages, of one type of system or solution with another, etc.). Preparation in this kind of question is essential because writing an answer without it, unless you are a very gifted writer or very practised waffler, will lead you into disastrous tangles and illogical consequences.

Make a table, in rough, headed FOR and AGAINST, into which you list the points and your conclusion. Then answer the question from your rough notes, expanding your conclusion in the final paragraph.

If you have ever done that most useful of all exercises, a précis, you will know that most paragraphs have a main topic. This is set out in a sentence usually placed at the beginning or end of the paragraph. The rest of the paragraph develops the theme by providing examples or facts. The theme of the paragraph you are now reading is that *paragraphs have a main topic*. The topic here is capsuled in the first sentence, and could have been capsuled in the first line. Change round the first sentence to begin with 'You will know ...' and end it with ... 'a prêcis," and note that the next sentence starts with "This ..." You should now realize why the main topic of the paragraph had to come not in the first but in the second half of the opening sentence.

In an examination essay, use the reverse of the précis technique by taking as topic sentences those points you have jotted down in rough. They provide the main gist of your argument. Develop them in the rest of the paragraph. Do not get alarmed at the amount of writing paper other candidates are using. Their handwriting may be larger than yours. But if you feel it absolutely vital to boost up your ego and depress the morale of other candidates by consuming vast quantities of paper, the following three tips may help: (i) Use wide margins at both sides of the paper; (ii) leave large spaces between each completed answer and (iii) write examples or illustrations downwards instead of across the page, e.g. .... There are the following points to consider:

Clarity
Brevity
Relevance

rather than. .... There are the following points to consider: Clarity, Brevity, Relevance.

Keep your sentences short. This is especially necessary if you come from a home background where standard English is a kind of second language, or if you do not shine in essay type examinations. Do not worry if short sentences make your work like a series of staccato gun shots. First things first. Can your writing be understood? Is your meaning clear? Fluency will come later.

Remember that an English essay, like a good feature article, should have an arresting opening, but tone down the opening if you are only answering essay-type examinations (as in History, Sociology, Law, British Constitution, Economics or Literature). In these examinations the examiner is interested in your knowledge and ability to impart it, not in your emotions. Answer formal questions in a formal style. They are designed to test not creativity but knowledge.

The English language becomes a vital, living thing by the infusion of new dialects and idioms. To be addressed by the Bank Manager as Honourable Miss or Master instead of Dear Sir or Dear Madam would certainly make life more colourful, but would we not wonder what kind of person was now in control of the bank?

So keep your native idiom for your creative writing. It will give you a personal style that cannot easily be copied and may well be envied. Think of the many writers overseas all of whom use English but who make of it something entirely individualistic to themselves and their countries. Read Chinua Achebe's *Man of the People*. Its humour, compassion and racy dialect could have come from nowhere else but Nigeria, yet it is written in English. Similarly with Cyprian Ekwensi's work or that of Amos Tutuola, or the beautifully written stories with an Indian background by R. Prawer Jhabvala. Contrast her character studies with those of E. M. Forster in *A Passage to India*. All of these writers use English, yet mould the language to their own styles as a potter fashions his clay.

When you have developed all your points, look back to the question again before penning your final paragraph. You should often refer to the question while writing an answer but in the excitement of the occasion, this is often forgotten. So now, at the last paragraph, check whether you have wandered from the subject a trifle. Let us hope it is only a trifle.

Summarize your arguments or emphasize your conclusions and make them obviously relevant to the question even to the extent of repeating its form in the last paragraph.

Finally, *theses and extended essays*. These are not competitive as are essay-type examination questions. Furthermore they have to be couched not simply as in other forms of communication, but in as complex a style as possible.

Frame a simple title in the most erudite terms you can think of. (Accepted by a University for a Master's thesis, I was chided jokingly by a tutor for giving it a title that anybody could read and understand. We spent some time on devising one that was barely intelligible.)

Write out pages upon pages of accurate but relevant facts in the dullest or most turgid language you can devise. Sprinkle footnotes throughout the text and add a lengthy bibliography which can easily be copied from other books. Include a list of contents or chapters, illustrations and of course appendices. Then get it typed, beautifully presented and even corrected for a few pounds by a professional typist.

Send her a bouquet when you receive your Master's or Doctor's degree. Having acquired half the alphabet behind your name and insulated yourself against those dull chores reserved for the 'unqualified', you can afford to be generous. Shed not your light around you, but your largesse.

CHAPTER 12

FEATURES

OUTLETS for short story writing may be dwindling but, fortunately for writers, the feature market continues to expand. It is not easy to define a feature article in a few words: it can be a 'think' piece about any subject an editor likes to print; it may be a factual piece of writing which differs from a news report only in being written more discursively, and in the hands of an expert, more imaginatively. It can be an article of 150 words, or it can be part of a series which may run for several weeks in a newspaper and draws jackpot fees of around £25,000.

But one thing is certain about the feature article: it offers more opportunities for the professional freelance as well as the beginner to writing than are available in almost any other field of writing. The outlet for short stories yearly narrows, the market for features continues to expand: Editors of over 100 Sunday and daily newspapers, 1,000 weekly newspapers, 2,000 general magazines and 2,000 trade magazines in Britain alone are looking for topics and styles that will appeal to their readers, draw attention to their magazines and merit block-buster advertising on the front cover.

The writer who can produce an original, well-written, factually accurate article which increases a man's knowledge of himself (or woman's of man's and all computations thereof) or of the world about him, will have no difficulty in earning not only his bread and butter but his jam, too, for many years to come.

'Think' or opinion pieces on current topics are usually wanted only from experts. When, however, a person feels deeply about a particular subject (the extension of the school leaving age, the permissive society, capital punishment, legal abortion, racialism, women's lib, etc.) and is able to communicate that passion intelligibly and convincingly he will usually be able to sell the resultant piece. What he will not be able to do is to make consistent sales from passion alone.

For continuing sales of freelance articles, facts must be allied to passion. *The Daily Telegraph* Colour Supplement publishes once weekly an 800-word Opinion Feature which prefaces the magazine. This is a good example of a 'think' piece. The emphasis is on controversy, and the normal payment is £50 or £60, although higher rates may go to writers whose names and opinions have the power to stir otherwise somnolent readers.

'How to . . .' articles always have a ready market in the Do-It-Yourself press, children's magazines and in feature articles of general papers. Here, tips for making articles of use in the home and worskhop are wanted, preferably with simple illustrations. Write the instructions in a logical sequence. Steer between the Scylla of assuming the reader to be a complete imbecile and the Charybdis of imagining him to know the exact meaning of every technical phrase you use.

A good exercise for learning the technique of writing 'How to—' articles is to imagine you are teaching somebody to drive a car. The first step to get it moving (assuming it is roadworthy and has sufficient petrol!) is to switch on the ignition. Don't say, open the door, or get into the car or find the key, etc., etc., because the instruction 1. Switch on the ignition, can only be carried out if the learner is in the car. But you may have to point out or illustrate where the ignition is and which way to turn the key.

Sometimes an opening for amusing aspects of family life can be carved out in the provincial press. Humour and advice in articles of under 500 words, arising out of practical experience are most in demand, but you are unlikely to make a rich living like this unless your talents are spotted by some national newspaper . . . a rather unlikely event. You must look to expanding markets. One of the biggest is the leisure industry.

Travel articles are part of this industry. The decrease in the number of hours worked per week means an increase in leisure and all those pursuits connected with leisure: D-I-Y, travel, sailing, gardening, embroidery, painting, sports, hobbies. As an indication of the phenomenal growth in the leisure industry, consider the following points.

The U.S. Department of the Interior Bureau of Outdoor Recreation, quoted in *Camping and Outdoor Life*, July, 1971, estimates that 40m. Americans spent 2,000 million dollars in 1970 on camping equipment, and it expects those figures to double by 1975. The U.S. Recreational

Vehicle Institute says that three million recreation vehicles are used in America today and estimates that this will increase to over seven million by 1980. The Dodge Truck Division of Chrysler increased its production of recreation vehicles 21 times between 1956 and 1966 from (15,000 units to 324,000). Ford say that more than 28 per cent of their annual car and light truck volume is for outdoor recreation vehicles (station wagons, cars for towing and trucks for camping units).

Camp-grounds of America have some 500 franchised sites in forty-six U.S. states, four Canadian Provinces and plan to open another twenty sites in Mexico in 1971.

These figures reveal a tremendous demand for packaged holidays and —more important to the travel writer, a demand for information about good places to visit, camp sites, and interesting routes. Lively informative features on all aspects of tourism and travel are always wanted. 'Think' pieces are a waste of time here. All the emphasis is on facts. Even if you are the dullest imaginable writer, but can give (however dully) information on interesting places you have visited, how you got there, where you stayed, the available amenities and the prices you paid, you will be welcomed by editors flaunting a cheque book.

Most daily newspapers run a Saturday leisure page that features items of travel interest, often by staff writers, but a space will always be open to the freelance with a new slant, new ideas or information. Markets other than the daily press are the women's magazines, and caravan and camping magazines listed in the *Writers' and Artists' Year Book*.

Sailing is another hobby that has greatly increased in popularity, probably because of the decreasing price of small boats. The number of magazines devoted to all aspects of the small boat industry has mushroomed in the last few years. A writer who has knowledge, particularly for the beginner, of what dinghy to buy, club to join, route to take, is in a fortunate position. If he can also write with a little humour, as lovers of small boats often can, he should have no difficulty in selling his work to any of the great variety of yachting/boating magazines that can be found in increasing variety on the bookstalls.

The bookstalls indeed provide the most important clue to current markets. The beginner who wants to specialize in features should constantly check on current titles of magazines and newspapers, the type of articles published. Hi-Fi, football, coins, motoring, antiques ... are all pursuits that have boomed in the last decade, and which now have a large number of magazines devoted entirely to those interests. Articles on all aspects of health care, including, nutrition and slimming are also on the increase. Indeed the writer who can communicate intelligibly and with affection about his own particular hobby or interest should have no difficulty in placing articles on his specialism.

'Do-it-yourself' features are a good way of beginning if your preference is for the succinct approach. This type of feature lends itself to simple illustration, and is in demand not only for D-I-Y magazines, but for the letter columns of general and women's magazines.

Finally, don't forget topicality. Features about tennis are more acceptable for printing in the summer, and ski-ing in December/ January, but should be submitted months earlier. Biographies of famous people are more avidly read on the occasion of their birthday or centenary, and descriptions of famous battles, or events have a greater fascination on the anniversaries of the dates when they happened.

And if you want to expand your expertise into a short length book, try some of the 25,000 word mini-books, such as the Corgi ones which publish a whole range of subjects from Yoga to Cat Care, Dieting to Dressmaking, Spelling to Antiques.

CHAPTER 13

THE RELIGIOUS PRESS

THE religious press offers one of the easiest markets of all to beginners. For this, and other reasons, it is among the worst paid. On one occasion I had to interview for a newspaper, the headmaster of a famous public school. I panted behind this huge man, surely the fastest, biggest mover to be seen off a rugby pitch. He raced round the school and showed me the whole works in about five minutes flat. Gasping for breath, I thanked him for his courtesy. As I staggered away, he landed a metaphorical body blow. "If you ever want to make money from writing," he said, "clear out of the religious press." He was an ordained priest.

His words sounded very harsh, but in them there was more than a grain of truth. Religious periodicals, like public services, are not motivated by the same ideas as commercial undertakings. The religious press has to run at a profit, otherwise it would go bankrupt, but its audience is often poor, or dispersed over large areas. Unlike a local or regional newspaper therefore, the religious presses cannot always avail themselves of the economies of large-scale production. Their distribution costs are higher, and their advertisement revenue, spasmodic. The bulk of it comes from advertisements for nannies or teachers, or apartments, the rest from appeals.

The beginner will therefore be surprised to learn, that in spite of all these disadvantages, the religious press can probably give him more opportunities than are to be found in almost any other field. But I admit to being biased. The first article I ever had published in a national weekly was in the religious press, at the age of 18. It gave me a real thrill to see not only my name but even my photo in a paper printed in Fleet Street. I thought I was made, and when letters actually reached me from odd places throughout the world as a result of the appearance of my article, I was sure that I was already far up on the ladder to fame and glory.

The first great advantage of writing for the religious press is perhaps strangely, the freedom to put a point of view in your own way. I am not saying you get the freedom to write anything. One cannot expect the arguments, if any exist, for a Sex Supermarket to be voiced in *The Church Times*, any more than one would expect an article on the mysticism of St. Teresa to appear in the communist daily, *The Morning Star*. But within the religious framework of the actual magazine, editors provide a great deal of freedom. You can state your case, write your story in your own words without alteration or 'editing'.

Secondly, if your story just falls short of publication standard, an event not so rare for a beginner, editors in the religious field are usually extremely helpful in telling you why. An article I once submitted to a religious newspaper came back to me: "Highly readable and much useful information, but for our readers, not enough *point*." Could anything be more helpful to an aspirant writer than cogent, succinct criticism like that? It was really worth a cheque in itself!

The third great advantage of the religious press to the beginner is that it provides him with a market while he is still an amateur. He can try for the letter pages, or the articles, or the short story. Avoid the parish pump style of writing, and never, for God's sake, preach.

The kind of material that religious weeklies and monthlies want varies as much as do the contents of different womens' magazines. As always, the best way of discovering editors' needs is to see what they publish. Though they all want articles and stories that appeal to Christian readers, the Christian reader appears in many disguises. He may be a disputatious theologian, a humble parishioner interested in Church attendance, social work and Lenten cookery, or a person with no sectarian beliefs but very concerned with social and moral issues: the underprivileged, the homeless, abortion laws, corporal punishment.

Writers for this market therefore have a wide field, and as in all writing, specialization pays. Find the niche that suits *you*.

1. Suggestions for features are interviews with famous Church personalities. Well-known people in the Church, unlike famous football or TV personalities, do not always get a good press. An interview or confrontation gives them a chance to redress the balance, and most churchmen will respond very courteously to a request for an interview even by a beginner.

Get background information. Look up *Who's Who* to find out how they are addressed, or ring up their secretaries, and ask. In writing, Rev. with Christian name or initials and surname is safe for almost all ordained ministers of religion in Britain, followed, if he is also a doctor, by the appropriate initials. 'Minister' can be used for most denominations, though Roman Catholics favour 'priest'. 'Father' is a colloquial form of address between R.C.s and is being used more frequently in writing, too. 'Parson', not acceptable to most denominations, is best avoided. Only the Church of England has a 'vicar' and a 'rector', so check, or refer to him as the 'minister' of . . . Church. In the Congregational Church a woman may be Rev. but in the Methodist and some other denominations a woman is a 'Deaconess' and described as 'Sister Phyllis Brown'. Roman Catholic nuns are also increasingly using this form of address. An unordained man can be described as a 'lay preacher', although in the Methodist church which has most of them, he is called a 'local' preacher to distinguish him from the ordained ministers who 'travel'.

Whenever you interview anybody it is tactful to find out what they have written . . . even if you cannot bring yourself to read it. Writers always respond more readily to interviewers who know something about their work.

The practice of printing an interview without the interviewee seeing the proof makes for controversial and lively journalism, but I have never been able to do it. and have always sent interview articles back to the source for agreement/correction before publication. For an aspirant writer, this is probably the best technique. You and your editor, are covered against most of the hazards including libel, though your writing may be watered down a bit and any uncomplimentary inferences removed. This tends to take the sting or bite out of an article and perhaps to make it less readable, but even within these limits one ought to be able to produce a recognizable pen portrait, even if it does suffer some of the defects of a Court painting.

2. Reporting meetings of interest to Christians can earn a little jam for a journalist's bread. A letter sent me by Count Michael de la Bedoyere during his editorship of the *Catholic Herald* sums up this art in an eminently clear fashion and there is nothing one can add to his exposition of the technique. He mentions photographs too, for it is helpful if would-be contributors to church magazines can supply

photographs of meetings or churchmen as such magazines often lack the funds to engage staff photographers.

"In reporting congresses, etc., it is rather important for us that you should not attempt a kind of summary of work studied but instead underline one or two outstanding and specially interesting matters that would be of particular interest in this country. When one writes that kind of story, it is often a help to think whether one has started it with a subject that can easily be headlined in a popular paper. In the same way, we are not interested in static pictures of bishops, priests, of which we have so many. We much prefer an 'action' picture, e.g. an interesting close-up of faces listening to the speeches—or a good scenic picture that relates to the congress or event. I know these are more hard to come by but anything like straight platform pictures are useless to us."

3. Topicality, as in all writing, adds to the acceptability of a feature or story. The aspirant writer should therefore arm himself with a liturgical calendar, a potted biography of famous saints and their feast days. Candlemas, Easter, Whitsun, Christmas . . . however dated these subjects appear, are the recurring themes in the Christian Church. Jewish, Muslim, Hindu and other sects have their own feast days, customs, and increasingly—the newspapers in which to write about them. Be prepared to do a little research and come up, if you can with something different, as for example the kind of coins that appear in collections during and after the summer holidays. But whatever the theme of your article, get the largest portion of your appeal in the first paragraph.

4. Travel articles are always welcome. Pictures and articles about famous shrines; places of pilgrimage; towns and villages where saints and martyrs lived will all find interested editors—and readers. Remember that with the occasional sad exception, there is a far greater oecumenical spirit in all churches today. Write therefore not from a sectarian but from a general viewpoint, emphasizing, when relevant, the unity of mankind, rather than their differences.

5. The market for 'religious' stories in an old narrow sense has dwindled almost to nothingness, but there is still an opening for stories usually with a family interest and of good moral tone. The pay is low, but half a loaf may be better than no bread to a starving journalist, and the beginner writer may prefer even a £3.15 cheque for a 1,000 word

story to an engraved rejection slip from a world-famous publishing house.

6. There are also the reward titles, undertaken by certain presses such as Lutterworth Press and Victory Press. Reward titles are books with wholesome themes likely to appeal to young readers, which are written for the Sunday school prize market. Though this is a dwindling market it is still quite active.

7. Parishes often publish a news letter. Many an overworked vicar or priest would be glad of help in preparing the news sheet or magazine and in typing or delivering them. These chores are not only helpful to the vicar but to the writer who does them. He will learn the news angles to emphasize and to avoid in writing a paper of local interest. He will learn also of the need to cram into a local report as many readers' names and activities as possible.

8. Having emphasized, perhaps unduly, the small rewards that go to beginner-writers of articles and stories for the religious press (established names of course get more), I must conclude with the rich rewards open to the man or woman who can weave a novel round a religious theme or plot. If you believe these are unreadable or out of touch with modern needs, think again. What about *The Devil's Advocate, Shoes of The Fisherman* or *Children of the Sun?*

Look at the continuous sales of Graham Greene's *The Heart of the Matter,* or *The Power and The Glory,* or Audrey Erskine Lindop's *The Singer Not the Song.* The latter is a particularly remarkable achievement in that the author draws such an authentic background of South America without ever having set foot there. She got all the details from her own research at home in England, coupled with the use of an exceptionally fertile imagination. (In this she is rather like Harry Patterson, a Leeds author with thirty books to his credit, and an income of £20,000 a year from adventure stories written under the name of Jack Higgins. Set in exciting places like China, Sicily, Mexico, Greenland and the Amazon, amidst teeming jungles full of murderous animals, serpents and men or on freezing ice caps, they move at a cracking pace. Yet Harry rarely moves out of his Yorkshire dales and never to the places he describes with such meticulous attention to detail in his books.)

If you think there is no money to be made in the religious field, ask yourself what best seller there is to equal the Bible. Film epics like *The*

Ten Commandments, *Ben Hur* and *Quo Vadis* drew millions more people to the cinema yesterday than any 'blue' film or X certificate does today. The person who can write with force and sincerity about moral problems, about human conduct and belief, who can describe credible characters and weave interesting plots against a religious background (like Lloyd Douglas in *The Robe*) is certainly going to reap rich rewards in this life and possibly in a life to come. What more desirable situation can a writer ask for than that?

CHAPTER 14

TRADE AND PROFESSIONAL MAGAZINES

I WAS once rung up by the editor of a well known trade journal and asked if I would write an article for his magazine. Journalists used to being rung up by editors, soliciting their favours, take this situation in their stride. It was the first time it had happened to me. The editor explained that he had seen my published work and felt I would be the right person for the job he had in mind. This was to describe the advantages and disadvantages of moving a factory and its work people from London to a new location.

Would I do it? Too flattered to think of refusing, or worse still ... even to ask what rates he paid, I agreed. The pay-off came to nearly £47, excluding expenses, for an article of 3,000 words, and this in 1956. The cheque taught me a lesson that I would otherwise never have found out: namely, that professional and technical journals are among the most remunerative fields of journalism for a writer to work in. Only recently I was asked to do a smaller piece for a shipping magazine which had links with the oil industry, and for 1,500 words I was paid £35.

Not every technical and professional magazine pays so highly. The beginner-writer must learn to distinguish between some which are barely able to balance their budgets, and those being subsidized by an industry, company, association, or rich advertisers.

A professional journal is one read and mostly written by members of a particular profession. It describes new trends and techniques; provides information of interest to members and associated bodies.

A technical journal treats of new developments in a particular industry; a trade journal features subjects and news items of interest to people in a particular trade: such as window displays, new chain store managers or methods of packaging. And then there are hybrids which combine features of them all. Is *Signature*, the magazine of the Diners' Club, a professional or technical journal? Similarly with *Drive*, the A.A. magazine, or *Giroscope*, the magazine of the Giro card holder, or *Barclaycard*, the magazine for holders of Barclay credit cards.

The subjects which appear in the technical and trade press are not exactly soul shattering. Writing a piece about "Plastic Packaging means Rindless Pigs" is not quite the creative writer's dream assignment. But a truly professional writer must regard such themes as a challenge. Even if there is no opportunity for the exposition of your exquisite descriptive powers, at least you'll get a handsome by-line and a cheque to match.

Furthermore this is likely only to be the beginning. Turning out a light-hearted piece of humour for a national daily and making it look as if the 150 words have been tossed off in minutes, takes considerable time and ingenuity. Then it will reap little more than £15, perhaps less for an unknown. Having produced this little masterpiece, it does not get you a freelance weekly spot for your amusing 'think' pieces even though the editor writes that he "would always be pleased to see more of your work without prejudice". Your markets have to be won over and over again in competition with the paper's own journalists who are likely to be among the best in the world.

By contrast the professional and technical press can provide a regular source of income for the person with professional or technical knowledge. The emphasis is always on expertise and accuracy. No accountants', bankers' or solicitors' journal wants out-of-date information. Opinions are welcome, but must be backed up by original research. Quotes must give the derivation of source material. Any writer who makes an incorrect allusion or gives an incorrect fact in a children's book will bring down a storm of (deserved) criticism upon his head. But readers of professional magazines will find inaccuracy so insulting to their intelligence that the offending writer will never be asked to contribute any further pieces ... unless he is a world famous name, and the editor has a superb proof reader. The beginning contributor should remember the old adage, 'When in doubt, leave out'.

Some readers get a vicarious thrill in spotting errors. Even a borrowed library book will not be immune to the pencilled comment from an irate reader who thinks he has spotted some contradiction or error in the text. I have such a book before me now. The title is *The Murder*

Squad of Scotland Yard by Gerald McKnight (W. H. Allen, 1967), and in the chapter dealing with 'The Constantine Butchers,' p. 67, occurs the line. . . "a police constable had been sent back inside to search. He had found both cigarettes and matches which could have belonged to William Rowe." A pencilled margin note says "See p. 59" Going back to p. 59 is the paragraph, "Willy shook his head. No, his brother had died of cancer. What was more, cancer was caused by smoking, and he did not believe in smoking."

I have quoted this pencilled notemaker because he (she?) is typical of the reader who spots anything that appears to be a discrepancy even in writing the function of which is primarily to entertain. If you want to make a living from the professional and technical press, accuracy, absolutely up-to-date reference sources, and fastidious attention to detail are prime requirements.

The professional magazines sometimes include articles for the more general reader. Thus *The Banker* publishes items of interest to the practitioner and the student of banking as well as to lay readers interested in monetary and economic affairs. *The Accountant* features items of interest for professional accountants and readers hoping to pass accountancy exams. *Drive* includes articles of general appeal as well as those of particular interest to the car driver or owner. This is likely to be a continuing development and one which will provide the observant freelance journalist with an increasing number of markets. The pay is uniformly good.

So if you have any kind of expertise or if you practise a trade or profession and cannot aspire to the daunting length of a book, do not ignore the technical magazines. Write, as always, about what you know. Slant it for the man who doesn't know but who could quite easily if you told him how.

CHAPTER 15

THE 'GIVE-AWAY' PRESS

F AR more people buy goods through the post today because of newspaper and magazine advertisements than they did even a decade ago. A new type of industry has mushroomed from this development: the mail order business. This is a method of selling by using literature distributed through the letter box, to persuade people to buy the goods or services described. The goods are distributed not only from well-known stores but also from central depots: a large warehouse or even a small terrace house in a back street.

The give-away press is one facet of the mail order trade. A circular in newspaper format, its size ranges from the 4-page *News Shopper* circulating in Croydon to the much larger *Focus on South-West London* which is delivered free to 280,000 homes in south-west London, and is purported to be read by a million readers.

Distributors of the give-away press are paid so much per 1,000 copies by the owners of the paper. Literary contributions are also paid for. How are papers able to pay these costs without charging anything for the paper? The answer is because of the revenue they earn from advertisements. Many of the articles published are geared to or triggered off by advertising needs. As an example I was asked to do a 1,500 word article on the opening of a new extension to a Health Food Shop. I interviewed the owner, got some idea of his background, facts about his new premises, and of the most popular items in his stock, and wrote the piece. It was featured in a middle page spread with the photo of the proprietor and his new shop premises. Around the report there was a large section of advertisements, all on health food or similar products. The person I had interviewed had paid the editor for advertisement space. The editor was paying me to write the article: in effect to do a Public Relations job. All the other advertisements had come into the office as a result of this special feature which drew attention to different types of health foods.

Another similar commission spread over four months was to write on housing with special reference to housing finance and grants under the Housing Finance Act 1969. The editor had seen that most of his advertisements came from builders, Do-It-Yourself shops, plumbing, roofing and glazing specialists ... all people connected with home improvement and maintenance. Hence I got a commission on housing which naturally attracted larger and bigger advertisements from everybody connected with the buying and maintenance of houses.

The greatest attraction of the give-away press for the beginner is in the chance it provides of consistent and regular sales. If one piece is submitted which the editor likes, he will commission more. As your writing and name become better known, you will be able to command better rates. You get regular sales and become known to a wider readership. There is one disadvantage ... namely, you are in effect acting as a P.R.O. and therefore cannot condemn the product, service or organization you are writing about. You have to see only what is good about it. This could be a very serious limitation for the polemic writer. On the other hand, it is wise to remember the dictum that the great film director Sam Goldwyn used to give script writers who wanted to use the film medium for protests or appeals. "If you want to send a message", he is reported to have said on more than one occasion, "use Eastern Telegraph."

If you like campaigning *against* people, products, situations, it might be wiser to ignore the outlets afforded by the give-away newspaper. So far, writing for this press has caused me no heart pangs at all. On the contrary I find it very acceptable to have two or three regular monthly commissions to turn out, plus constant 1,500 word assignments on topics as varied as German fruit juices or house improvement grants.

Some give-away newspapers employ no outside staff. They run on a shoe-string budget with two full time workers: an editor-writer and a secretary, usually the editor's wife. If you get no response when you send in an article to a give-away paper, rejection is not a reflection on the quality of your writing. It is more likely to indicate the illiquid structure of the paper's finance. Try a controversial letter instead. If it arouses enough interest, the editor may be able to follow it up with a 100–250 word article on some similar subject. Make suggestions for articles which are a form of advertising such as wining and dining at restaurants in the area covered by the paper with a write up of the meal afterwards. Even if you only get a free meal for yourself (and preferably friend, too) and the article is unpaid, the cost of an evening's meal nowadays can rise to astronomical heights, and a free meal is not to be sneezed at by the impecunious writer.

Other suggestions which may meet with an editor's approval are travel articles which take up little space; places of local interest; discs, write-ups on local films and plays ... anything that can be geared to advertising, for this is the give-away editor's lifeblood and without it he cannot function at all.

During the summer months articles on any aspect of weddings become very acceptable to editors because again these can be geared to advertisements from caterers, photographers, dress hire, and a whole range of other products and services of interest to prospective brides, grooms, relatives and friends.

Brush up or develop any specialism within your powers; this can be a great asset in journalism if you can adapt it to popular taste. I have an economics qualification earned at Oxford many years ago. Readers of a general paper are not interested in economics as an academic subject, but many readers are interested in money, how to get it, spend it, save it. I have aimed therefore to make the most of an economics background by writing comment on money matters such as insurance, taxation, investment. Each of these subjects is a specialism in itself but in writing 500 words on finance for a monthly give-away paper, one does not have to be in the same class as Keynes expounding his *General Theory of Employment*.

The editor of a give-away paper has no fixed ideas about what readers want. His job is to encourage advertisers to take space in his paper. Anything that makes his magazine more attractive to readers, and more widely read, interests him. If he thinks your work is likely to get him more advertisers, he will consider any kind of story or article from you. His tastes are among the most catholic of all editors. Give-away papers can't pay Fleet Street rates, as my own editor constantly reminds me, but they do give the talented beginner three very big advantages:

(i) a very wide range of possible articles and stories
(ii) the chance to develop a specialism, and
(iii) the opportunity to notch up consistent sales.

CHAPTER 16

THE CHILDREN'S MARKET

ONE of the most rewarding fields for the creative writer to work in is the children's market. By rewards I do not mean the ability to earn the same royalties as Malcolm Saville or other children's writers who have reached the pinnacle of success, but the rewards which come to even the most amateur writer in this field: namely a following of devoted readers who, strange as it may seem, will love your stories and characters, and will write and tell you so in no uncertain terms. Furthermore, providing your books keep in print, or your output continues, you will find no lack of readers: babies are constantly being born, growing up and—like schools—looking for reading material.

It is a popular myth that writers try the children's market because it is easy. Don't believe it. The competition is enormous, and becoming more so. The readership, where facts are concerned, is highly critical, and you have to supply action, action, action, even if for the younger reader, it is only domestic action, all the way.

Don't think you can use the juvenile market as a stepping stone to adult fiction. You can't. The techniques are quite different. Famous writers are sometimes asked to turn out a book for young adults, mainly because of the power of their names and their writing skill. But few keep in the field for long. Adult novels have the chance of reaching the jackpot, being filmed, televised and all the rest. Save for the exceptionally talented or lucky writer, peripheral advantages in writing juvenile literature are few. However, they are growing. There is the paperback revolution in children's literature which fosters a mass market. Subsidiary rights can be earned by TV adaptations, or the production of toys based on characters in children's books.

But there are certain obvious restrictions in writing for children. You must discipline yourself to write simply, to introduce and sustain plenty of action. You must not indulge in philosophical

88

speculations (though moral teaching is still very acceptable) or flights of literary fancy and finally (and most difficult of all) you must not forget the age group for which you are writing. This means producing a uniform style. Otherwise, as the book proceeds, you will become so carried away that whereas Chapter One can be taken in almost by a five-year-old, the last chapter may read like a Ph.D. thesis.

In spite of these limitations there is something particularly gratifying in writing for young people. Even a story of book length can sometimes be tossed off fairly quickly because it rarely exceeds 60,000 words, and is often much shorter. The material you create can be used at bedtime or playtime for your own children, and no matter whether your stories are noticed by a reviewer or not, some child will have gained pleasure and extended the boundaries of his imagination by what you have written.

Furthermore he will prove it by buying your books. Enid Blyton's work has sometimes been condemned by literary critics. One library even banned her works (mainly because of their popularity.) But when I see children spend their whole week's pocket money for a book by this author, this seems to be the accolade of any writing career, and a far greater tribute than any literary award.

The first point to notice about writing for the children's market is that it is vast. There are ample, but highly competitive, opportunities for beginners. The market comprises books of all kinds, including teenage romance, science fiction, history, general education, animal stories (especially horses) and adventure. There is also a large output of comics and weekly papers catering for younger children.

The writer who wants to begin in the children's market by writing articles or short stories should buy copies of 6–12 different types of magazines and study them. Remember that many adult magazines such as the *Nursery World*, have paragraphs or supplements for children, and there is the term-time magazine *Everyweek*.

Be prepared to try anything: plays, stories, articles, songs, things to make-and-do ('activities') puzzles. There are two reasons for not specializing too early. One is to find out what you can sell most readily, and the other is that to make a living from juvenile writing you must write much and often.

Keep records of rejections and any comments from editors. Try local papers. Ask them if they would like a Children's Page. Send a sample of your work. Regular commissions keep the baying of wolves from the door and facilitate the move into full-time freelancing.

If you can produce marketable work regularly, try a syndicate. They may be able to give you world-wide publication. Addresses are in the *Writers' and Artists' Year Book*. If you part with only the First British Serial rights, this means that six weeks after publication you are free to sell the same material again anywhere in the world.

But it is in books, fiction and non-fiction, where the biggest material rewards are to be gained. You do not need the same amount of expertise as you might for an adult text book, but you must research for new and interesting material. Do not lose sight of the fact that it is a highly critical audience and that children like to put ideas to the test of practical experience. You will also have to learn, if you do not already know, how to write brightly and simply. It is a very good discipline for the turgid, complex or wordy writer to write children's books. And there is the huge market of children's educational books, general and specialized.

It is wise to send a MS. out several times, and for longer MSS, articles and stories up to 5,000 words, this pays off. I am not so sure about books, even after reading that this or that author had his work rejected *x* number of times, and then went on to become a success. But I am biased and the following story may show why.

A publisher asked me if he could send a children's novel I had submitted to him to a film company he knew. If they took it, he would publish the book. Two previous publishers had seen the book, both sending it back with comment and criticism (One: "marvellous dialogue but the characters never come alive," The other: "the characters are very real . . . but.")

The film company then wrote to me saying they liked the book very much. The characters were good; the dialogue excellent. A few months later came a report that the book had been short-listed with two others for "possible filming next year". When that time came, I "would be paid for the book, and a much larger sum for collaborating on the film script". Six months later the book was returned . . . with a marvellous letter, but no contract. It had been rated as excellent for filming, but too much of the action took place outdoors, and so made shooting too costly for the limited resources of this particular company which specialized in making children's films. To have filmed the story indoors "would have altered its appeal".

The publisher who had introduced my work to the film company, and whom I'd never met, did not now wish to publish. After altering the novel back and forth to suit the needs and comments of the half a dozen subsequent publishing houses to which it was sent, and all in vain, I gave up in despair. The moral is, I suppose, to have absolute and unshakeable faith in your work, whether it is a children's or adult novel. Don't alter it at all, unless you are reasonably sure that when you have done so, you will have a guaranteed market. If you keep altering it first to suit one person and then another, you finish up by pleasing nobody, least of all yourself.

There is one other lesson that can be learned from this story, relevant to the marketing of TV or film scripts, namely that as a beginner you are more likely to sell if your set is small and cheap (a telephone box, park bench) and your number of characters few and easily identifiable. But television rights and film scripts don't usually fall into the lap of the beginner. If they do, he . . . or more likely she, has other talents far outside the scope of this book.

Writers who are prolific in ideas or output but do not know how to market their work, may wish to use the services of an agent. A list of literary agents can be found in the *Writers' and Artists' Year Book*, but they are becoming almost as selective as publishers. Some will not take on new clients at all without a recommendation from a writer already on their lists. One large agency estimates it can sell only 0·3 per cent of MSS. submitted by unestablished authors.

All agents appear to specialize. Some are interested primarily in theatre, television and broadcasting rights. Others give their major concern to overseas and translation rights. Some deal exclusively in serial stories and romantic fiction, others accept educational manuscripts. None appears to concentrate solely on the juvenile market while some specifically exclude children's books; also articles and short stories. A few agencies will undertake revision of work submitted to them by promising writers who have not yet been published. If payment is suggested for this task it will be in addition to the commission charges, which are around 10–20 per cent of the fee obtained from the sale of the author's work in a specified form, usually First British Serial Rights. This means a licence to publish in a particular form for a particular period. If the original work is adapted for another medium, such as television, a new right will be created which can be sold on behalf of the author. In Britain, seventy-five per cent of authors' output goes through the hands of five agents. Curtis Brown is one of the largest, A. P. Watt, the oldest.

The best advice regarding agents is to approach one with your own particular problems and to ascertain not only whether they will accept you but whether they will be of help to you personally either by helping to place your work in the most advantageous market, revising it to publication standard, or suggesting publishers who might be interested in your ideas.

Finally, a word about art work. This can be sold in the children's book world, additionally to or separately from MSS. submitted. Good book jacket designs as well as illustrations are wanted. Some artists like Ardizzone have already made a name for themselves in the world of children's books (*Tim All Alone*, etc.).

The Library Association's Kate Greenaway Medal may prove an additional incentive, for it is awarded annually to the artist who, in the opinion of the Library Association, has produced the most distinguished work in the illustration of children's books. Reproduction is taken into account when making the award. Artists who are interested even only as a temporary measure in illustrating their own books or jacket covers need only send samples of their work in the first instance. The ability to write and illustrate superbly well is a rare talent, but it is possessed by some: Mervyn Peake is an example. However, you may find yourself being acceptable to publishers as artist *and* author, a unique situation. Make the most of it!

CHAPTER 17

FICTION

THE first, but not the easiest outlet for the writer of fiction, is the novel. If a person has enough staying power to complete a book length story, and even two or three, literary success of some kind should surely catch up with him some day. But the early struggle may be very hard. The novel is becoming a very competitive market. Out of every 1,000 manuscripts submitted only one is likely to be accepted.

As an example of this competition the publishers, Secker and Warburg, publish 100 new titles a year of which less than half are fiction. The fiction side proves profitable only because the rewards on a few best-sellers more than balance the unprofitable first novels. And this is true of most publishers' lists.

The best way to begin in the most difficult field of novel writing (unless you are one of those amazing people who can turn out plots with the ease of a spider creating its web) is to write a synopsis first. Submit it with three specimen chapters to a publisher. If the writing is good and the synopsis full enough, the publisher will rush madly after you promising to make nearly all your dreams come true.

Alternatively, keeping well back in the safety of his office, he will mutter a few non-committal phrases or even an encouraging word or two. Either reaction is good enough for the author to persevere with his work to a conclusion. The third, and most likely possibility, is that he will send a letter of rejection, or even a printed slip.

In this case the only advice one can offer the disconsolate would-be author is to read the lives of other writers, their trials and failures. This will provide him with encouragement, help him to analyse his own writing aims once more (see Chapter I), and to consider how much he is prepared to sacrifice to achieve those aims.

As an example, take a look at the life story of playwright Eugene O'Neill. His brother James died in a sanatorium. His eldest son by his first wife (who himself married and left two wives) committed suicide

93

in his 30's. His daughter, Oona, married at 18 years, the 54-year-old film star Charles Chaplin, against Eugene's wishes. His son by a second wife had a son who died tragically at only two months. The son later became incapable of work and had to live on his wife's legacy inherited from her mother (murdered by the stepfather). The ex-husband of Eugene's third and last wife, Carlotta Monterey, committed suicide barely three days after they arrived back in the States from a long sojourn abroad.

Would a life history like that compensate you for creating *Mourning Becomes Electra*? Of course not all talented people have tragic lives, but it often needs very great talent indeed to overcome personal hardships and rise to the top in a chosen career. When the chosen career is in the world of art or entertainment the effort to reach the top may need great reserves not only of talent but of endurance. Sometimes a lower peak must be settled for, in order to effect a compromise between the heights that can be scaled happily and those that may take all the climber's resilience and strength. Perhaps the Spanish proverb sums up the position most succinctly: "Take what you want, says God, but pay."

Edgar Wallace, illegitimate son of small-time actress Polly Richards, and one of the most prolific writers of all time, was left as a small child to be brought up by a Billingsgate family with ten children. His early years were hard and fame came to him only by the expenditure of tremendous energy and an output so prodigious that people used to speak of the 'weekly Wallace' or even the 'daily Wallace'.

One week-end at his country house, Chalklands, he dictated a full length novel, *The Devil Man*. Beginning Friday night, he took a few hours' sleep on Saturday and again Sunday till noon. Aided in his waking hours by continual cups of tea brought by a servant on duty all night for this purpose he finished by 9 a.m. Monday, the 80,000 word novel about Charles Peace.

One January he arranged for four completed novels to be handed into his publisher . . . and two the next month. Yet when he died in 1932 his assets were almost nil, and the claims of his creditors £140,000 (paid —such are the rewards of posthumous fame—within two years).

He never forgot or forgave his early hardships. His mother (whose only other child, an older daughter, married and died in her twenties) contacted Edgar in his later life. The meeting was not repeated. She collapsed a few months later while touring with a company in Bradford. Removed to the Infirmary, she died there, uninsured and penniless, in November of the same year. She was saved from the final ignominy of being buried 'by the parish' only by the generosity of her ex-son-in-law. He had not kept much in touch after he remarried, but visited her in hospital, arranged for her to be buried in Catholic ground and sent her prayer book as a relic to her son, then in Canada.

Edgar, having so much, could spare no pity for the widowed mother who had borne him and who, in days long before the Welfare State and the permissive society eased the rearing of illegitimate children, kept and presumably cherished her child at least during his baby years. But all the rewards of Edgar's literary fame did not soften the bitterness which welled up within him whenever he thought of his 'abandonment'.

At the beginning of his great fame and wealth, he and his wife, for whom he had broken his first engagement, parted. One Christmas Eve at a bleak Swiss railway station, she handed over their younger son to spend his Christmas holidays with Edgar, his new wife 20 years his junior, and their family. As she watched the train drawing out with its load of happy holiday makers, leaving her alone on the deserted station, she experienced a wave of desolation so intense that she wandered about for hours afterwards almost in a state of hysteria. When some time later she died of cancer, Edgar could not bring himself to visit her and got progress reports from their two children.

Achieving literary fame and wealth does not always bring happiness to authors . . . sometimes it is the reverse for themselves and those about them. Edgar Wallace was a literary success: of that there is no doubt. Germany has produced nearly twenty films from his stories; there have been 39 TV films on the *Four Just Men* theme, 78 of his titles are still in print and his current annual sales some 40 years after his death are at $1\frac{1}{4}$ million copies. But happiness—?

To find out what it was like to live with another literary genius, read Stanislaus Joyce's wonderfully sympathetic biography of his talented brother James; of James's early struggles and later effort to keep with him his so dearly loved schizophrenic daughter in days when the treatment of mental illness was terrifyingly inhumane.

Another good biography for the writer to read is that of Joseph Conrad who found that trying to write, and even worse the inability to write at all, brought him to an abyss of despair from which he was saved only by the practical realism of his wife, Jessie. Ask yourself whether the ethereal and almost melancholy philosophy of Hardy's novels and poetry was in any way occasioned by his marriage to his first wife, Emmie? Though he separated from her, he could not marry again until after her death when he was 72 years of age.

Read the life stories of O. Henry, Ring Lardner, F. Scott Fitzgerald, Oscar Wilde, Jack London, and after you have done so, ask yourself, is this writing game really worth the candle? If you feel you must go on, then you'll reach the pinnacle one day, even if a couple of hundred rejection slips strew your path to the summit.

Meanwhile cheer yourself up with 'success' stories like that of playwright Sean O'Casey and his wife Eileen. She first fell in love with his *Juno and the Paycock*, met and married the author within sixteen months, and so began a domestic partnership that lasted for thirty-seven years until Sean's death in 1964. Or there is the story of Evan Hunter who gave up his high school teacher's job and became a telephone seller of lobsters for he could find no editorial work after months of searching. He submitted MSS. regularly to magazines all over the United States, received countless rejection slips and not a single acceptance until Scott Meredith's Literary Agency, in which he finally found a job to his liking, sold one of his stories for $12.60. Today, he can command half a million dollars for a novel before he puts pen to paper.

The second main outlet for the writer of fiction is the short story. This is the medium that beginners generally attempt, leaving the longer length of the novel for the more ambitious or more energetic writer.

A short story shows a character in conflict and his solution to the problem. Read some short stories and see whether they fit this definition. See how the theme of 'wasted' effort in Maupassant's *The Necklace* is used also in *The Juggler* of Anatole France but with a totally different conclusion.

Contrast Somerset Maugham's craftsmanship and worldliness with the equally impeccable craftsmanship, but different backgrounds of Katherine Mansfield. Read Saki's malicious tales about aunts and children and animals, or Salinger's about young people (*Franny and Zooey*; *For Esme with Love and Squalor*). Read Muriel Spark for the wonderful zany quality of her writing, her apparent lack of compassion, her mordant humour; Malamud and Bellow for their understanding particularly of Jewish characters; Jean Rhys for her simplicity and the haunting quality of sadness in her work; L. P. Hartley's *The Go-Between* or Graham Greene's *The Basement Room* for the ability to depict adults through a child's eyes.

James Joyce's stories of Dublin create a picture of the city and its people so real you can almost see them. Try, if you are not an addict already, science fiction. And if S.F. conjures up visions of moonmen only, begin with C. S. Lewis's *Perelandra* and *The Silent Planet* and go on to read *Flowers For Algernon* by D. Keyes. The technique of telling this story in the first person in the form of a diary is absolutely magnificent, but will not be appreciated until you reach the end. No wonder this compassionate story was made into the film, *Charlie*. No wonder when the author was awarded the Hugo prize for science fiction and asked how he had managed to produce such a story, his only reply was that if he knew how, he'd do it again.

Reading biographies of other writers reveals the trials and tribulations as well as the rewards of creative fiction, and provides you with motivation and encouragement. But reading the products of other writers, their features, short stories and novels, teaches you a little about plot, technique and style.

In a short story you will invariably find a character with whom you can identify faced with a problem which he (logically) resolves. If you find it hard, as beginners invariably do, to differentiate between an incident and a plot, remember that a plot is basically (1) a lead character (2) having to do something (3) which he cannot (4) because of psychological or physical obstacles, but (5) resolving the problem by (6) some logical solution. In other words, a story *moves* by the overcoming of the obstacles to a satisfying conclusion whereas an incident describes an event or happening, but unlike a story, without moving to any conclusion. A good example covering the points outlined above is the prize-winning *Ten Minutes on a June Morning* by Francis Clifford. First published in *Argosy*, it was reprinted in John Creasey's *Mystery Bedside Book*, 1971, the anthology of the Crime Writers' Association, edited by Herbert Harris, himself the author of nearly 3,000 short stories.

But however wide your reading of short, or long, stories, it will teach you little about selling. Today, this is a specialism in itself.

Though collections of short stories are consistently on loan from public libraries, outlets for the short story, so we are told, are rapidly diminishing. The beginner who wants to get published must therefore realize that the first essential is to study the market in depth.

The best selling opportunities today are to be found in the women's magazine market. English stories usually relate an incident or episode. James or Richard returns from an executive mission to tell the heroine he loves her, or doesn't. Plot, when it exists at all, is of the sketchiest. Characters tend to be drawn from one social class. The heroes are usually professional men, but not teachers, much given to travel. Manual workers of any kind, rarely make an appearance, and all the female characters seem to be compounded of an extraordinary mixture of sexual naïvety and sophistication.

Children, except in magazines emanating from Scotland, where readers must be either more tolerant or more realistic, are as rare as manual workers, save for the very occasional story in which they are the central figure around which the 'plot' revolves.

But allowing for this stylized format, which is very much looser in America (where both standards and rewards are so much higher), the women's magazine field still provides good openings for the short-story writer, expert and beginner. Even within the stylized form, different approaches are possible. These can range from the *True Confession*, to stories like *The Daughters* which appeared in *Woman's Journal*, and shows Muriel Spark at almost her talented best.

Even if, as the pessimists declare, the short story market is dwindling, opportunities are expanding in some spheres. One of them is the Confession market.

The Confession or True Story magazine reflects changing social attitudes on sex, religion, morals. Within the Confessions there are several sub-divisions. Some, particularly those imported from America, hover on the edge of pornography when they don't collapse into it altogether. The covers are lurid, leaving little to the imagination. They blazon titles like "I Married Into a Nudist Group" or "My Daughter Married My Lover" as well as answers to sex problems that can surely exist only in the robust mind of the magazine's 'resident' doctor.

When considering the rewards of this field, analyse carefully how important payment and publication are to you. Never, never, be fooled by those who tell you that the written word has no effect on human action, on the proclivity to evil or good. Why write, why publish? Has the Bible meant nothing ... or the Communist Manifesto? Have you never been moved by an appeal, a story, your imagination never been stirred by 'thoughts that lie too deep for tears'? Have you never been privileged to share with a poet his ear for rhythm, his personal vision? Of course the written word affects the reader ... even if it causes him to read instead of doing something else. So ponder well before your typewriter!

Most of the confession stories produced in Britain appeal to, and are usually related by, teenagers. Some are geared to the young marrieds. Market research is essential for success. Buy or beg copies of the magazines you aim to write for. Note that while narration is almost invariably in the first person, the age and sex of the narrators differ. There is always a demand for the *young* or teenage narrator because most of the readers of the confessions are young. Indeed during a spell of teaching in a comprehensive school, I found the girls so addicted to this type of reading that they tried little else. An older narrator lessens the chance of publication.

Plot in the staider English confession market tends to be of two types: sin, suffer and repent, in which the heroine commits some wrong, suffers for it and then repents. She becomes a reformed character and everything works out to a comparatively happy ending. The second type is the 'come to realize' in which the heroine doesn't sin but 'comes to realize' a defect in her character which is spoiling her chances of marriage, or creating grief and tension for her family (mother/husband/children), or unhappiness for her boss/workmates. She gets rid of the defect and lo, all is happiness and light once more.

Pay in the confession markets is fairly low to start with, but editors are very encouraging to anyone with a hint of promise and eventually you may be able to dictate your own pay. I have met many apparently quite ordinary young housewives who, by specializing in one type of story, the romantic, the light thriller or the confession, make themselves four-figure incomes while bringing up a family. But it takes perseverance, research, luck and of course, talent.

Don't attempt to write for confession or any other magazines if you think their content is 'below' you. You are writing for a very vulnerable reader: the impressionable teenager. Give them the best you've got.

The other type of fiction which is worth a mention because it sells so well in so many forms, is the crime or adventure story. Here, everything is subservient to the action, or to the working out of the plot. Characterization, a perennial element in the greatest novels, takes second place. There are exceptions. Read John Le Carré's *The Spy Who Came in From the Cold*, for its beautifully worked out plot, the realism of its background, the credibility of its characters. Or try *A Kiss Before Dying* by Ira Levin (author of *Rosemary's Baby*) for tension and compulsive readability, or Denis Wheatley for action.

Even Shakespeare is not averse to the lure of the detective story. Read *Henry VI*, Part II, Act 2, Scene 1, lines 59–160, beginning with "Enter Townsman of St. Alban's crying 'A Miracle'", and ending with a speech by Gloucester . . . "from whence they came." Who plays the detective and who the ineffectual companion, and what are the clues?

Because the detective or adventure story usually has an emphasis on *structure*, on the way the plot unfolds, on the building up of tension, a person who is skilled in the devising of plots and puzzles may be able to write a very acceptable adventure or crime story even if he is not a 'literary' writer, or one who is particularly gifted in the use of words.

Once when tidying up a student's room, I came across a printed card with the devastating words, HOLD ME TIGHT BABY, I'M YOUR LINK WITH THE ACTION. . . . words a writer of crime or adventure stories would do well to remember. For if he wants to produce good stories in this genre, he must be the reader's link with the action. Without action or the solution of a problem in the most devious yet logical way the writer can invent, a crime or adventure story is only worth reading if it comes from the pen of a master. And if a beginner is going to claim that title, why is he reading this book?

178778

CHAPTER 18

NON-FICTION: BOOKS

EDUCATION is expanding rapidly. In all countries there is an increasing desire and need for the accumulation and diffusion of knowledge. Books, films, radio and other media which can satisfy these wants are eagerly bought and borrowed by a vast public. The person who writes for this market should be assured of an appreciative audience and a good income for years to come.

First take text books. Whereas an average novel sells about 3,500 copies, even an average text book can go into several editions. Furthermore to boost earnings there are subsidiary rights in the form of tape recordings, an increasingly popular learning aid in developing countries. A text book writer's earnings may well therefore exceed those of a best selling novelist, though without his acclaim and literary prestige.

At an authors' meeting some years ago, I sat next to a young schoolmaster, named Ronald Ridout. Dissatisfied with the English book he was using in his own classroom, he tried to create a better one. So successful was his effort that his English Language schoolbooks now sell over two million copies a year, while the sales of his *English Today* have topped the five million mark.

Charles Eckersley, one time English master, did likewise. He realized that there were vast numbers of foreigners who wanted to learn English. Using his experience as a teacher in a polytechnic catering for foreign students, he produced *Essential English for Foreign Students* which is still selling in thousands, and has reaped for him rich rewards.

Other examples of successful text books spring readily to mind: Hall and Knight's *Algebra*, first published in 1885, is still selling.

The beginner to the text book field has a very good chance of earning useful and, with luck, even astronomical sums if (i) he is responsive to the needs of a particular market (ii) he can write with expertise and affection about his subject and (iii) he can make his subject, however erudite, intelligible to the layman.

Teachers are in a very fortunate position when it comes to text book writing. They know what is wanted by students. They have to organize and re-arrange the material they teach from year to year, and such notes can fairly easily be slanted for text book writing. The only snag for most full-time teachers is that by the time they have finished teaching they are too exhausted to write.

As well as text books there are reference books that can be produced by the writer with good ideas and skills in sequencing or synthesizing material. Roget's *Thesaurus*, first appeared in 1852, and is still going strong. The author's grandson was able to draw the royalties on the *Thesaurus* during his lifetime, and when he died in 1952, left house and property worth, £98,000. Fowler's *Modern English Usage* first published in 1925, sells, in revised editions, 20,000 copies each year.

Percy Scholes, music master and later critic, collected information and cuttings about music and musicians until he had enough for *The Oxford Companion To Music*, a monumental work with more than a million words and over 100 illustrations. In constant demand by students, musicians and libraries, the book is reprinted year after year. The knowledge Dr. Scholes gained while preparing this book helped him to write articles on music and to complete in ten days, *The Listener's Guide To Music*.

In 1954, Sir Hugh Beaver, managing director of the brewery firm of Guinness, could not find any reference book or encyclopaedia that gave an example of the fastest, fattest, leanest bird . . . or indeed animal or human, on record. Other records too that might be wanted by the seeker after odd superlatives, were equally difficult to find. Sir Hugh was introduced to the twin brothers Norris and Ross McWhirter who had their own research agency. They became editors of a new publication, *The Guinness Book of Records*.

First published in 1955, this extraordinary compilation of the biggest, oldest, littlest and other superlative records, reveals by implication how extraordinary a creature is man. It has sold over 7 million copies in 16 years. Save for the Bible it is the fastest non fiction seller in the world; is published in 14 countries and 12 languages, and is brought up to date every year.

Could *you* dream up an idea like that?

If not, what about travel? Have you specialized knowledge about a particular part of the world, its customs, scenic beauties, hotels? Could you write a reference book for the traveller? You can find successful examples of such books in any booksellers or stationers.

Or what about biography, another rich market for the non-fiction writer? Is there an historical character for whom you feel some affinity, about whom you could write an accurate yet readable story? Biographies have a universal appeal and often become the subject of films. A typical example is *Nicholas and Alexander* by Robert K. Massie.

In his introduction to this most readable book, Massie explains how he came to write it. Discovering that his own son had haemophilia, he tried to find out how other families had coped with the problems raised by this strange disease. The search led him to one of the most famous haemophiliacs of all, Alexis, fifth child and only son of Nicholas II, last Tsar of the Russian empire.

The arrival of this much wanted and prayed for heir, combined with his terrible genetic inheritance, was one of a series in a chain of events and consequences that led to the apparent assassination of the whole family, and subsequently to the Communist Revolution. Massie's researches resulted in the production of an enthralling biography of over 550 pages and a film which, in spite of the 'stars' being all unknown and all the major characters coming to a violent end, proved very moving and compassionate.

Perhaps some event or person in history has stirred *you*? Could it become a biography or a history book?

Are you any good at any of the sciences? The ability to write intelligibly about scientific or technical subjects is a rare talent. You may possess it. Try your hand at writing a book on that branch of science or technology in which you are an expert. A publisher or agent will soon confirm—or reject—your suspicions that you have the ability to produce a saleable book . . . If he turns you down, cheer up, he could be wrong. Try again.

Many people during the course of their lifetime acquire knowledge which can be used as the basis of a non-fiction book. Housewives have practical experience of general and sometimes specialized cookery: of cake-making, vegetarian diets, soups, meals for invalids or large families. Gardeners gain knowledge of the habits of annuals and perennials, of pests and pesticides. Skilled hairdressers or engineers learn tips and information about their trade which they can pass on to apprentices.

All these groups and many more acquire knowledge which can form the nucleus of a non-fiction book. What is the best way to begin writing the book and finding a market?

First ask a publisher to send you a copy of his current list of titles. Study these carefully. Is there a subject not yet covered or in preparation which you could tackle? Look at the backs of books. ... The forthcoming and current titles in a series are often printed there. Have you an idea for a text book which could fit in with that series?

As an illustration of this marketing technique, my youngest son one day brought home from the junior library a book called *All About the Sinking of the Bismarck* by Quentin Reynolds. He is not an avid reader, save of science fiction, so when I saw how this book was holding his interest, I borrowed it and found it a most enthralling narrative. On the back cover of the book were titles of others in the same series: *All About Dinosaurs, Football, King Arthur*, etc. I teach the unusual combination of English and Economics, but there was nothing in the published list into which either of these subjects would fit, for on closer analysis it could be seen that all the titles were about tangibles. But one branch of economics is concerned with money, which is a tangible, so I suggested a book *All About Money*. This title was just being considered when I wrote in, and no author's name had yet been thought of. After submitting a synopsis and a couple of chapters I was commissioned for the job. Luck operated for me on this occasion. The title might have already been considered and abandoned, or an author might have already been approached, and agreed to do the work. Fortunately neither had happened and the way was clear for me.

The steps to be taken to break into the textbook field can be summed up as follows: (i) Study publishers' lists. Note particularly any series that are being issued.

The chances of an idea for a book being taken up are more likely in a series, and sales for an unknown author are likely to be higher than in a one-off effort, for each book is a repetitive advertisement for others in the series. (ii) Think of a title which fits in with the publisher's current and forthcoming output. (iii) Make a synopsis of your prepared book, i.e. a list of chapter headings and a summary of their contents. (iv) Submit to the publisher of your choice, the synopsis with one to three fully written chapters, working from the simple to the complex, the known to the unknown. If the publisher needs further chapters to make up his mind, he will ask for them. (v) Give an estimate of the total number of words on the title sheet, i.e. the sheet which prefaces your MS. with title and author's name and address. Diagrams and photographs, if any, can be discussed later. (vi) if the book isn't to be part of a series, suggest to the publisher the market you have in mind, e.g. craft or apprentice students of engineering; postgraduate economic students; lay readers wanting to improve their culinary skills; commerce or typewriting to C.S.E. or R.S.A. standards. (vii) Enclose with the synopsis and completed chapter(s) enough stamps for the return of the work. The publisher didn't ask to see it, so do him at least the courtesy of stamps for his reply.

Some people suggest that it is wiser to say nothing about your background and let your book chapters and synopsis speak for themselves. But the fact that you are a professor of economics, or a teacher of typewriting, or a hospital nurse, or the mother of twelve children, can all be relevant to certain types of books for such facts increase your publication chances and the number of books that will be sold. The crux of any autobiographical details is will they increase sales? If they won't, leave them out.

What are the rewards? If only 5,000 copies of a text book are sold, not a very high number, and the book costs £1.50, a fairly low price, then royalties at 10 per cent will amount to £750, which for perhaps six months' effort may not be in the class of the Beatles' earnings. But writing the book will teach you something about the craft of writing which, added to your specialism, may land you, too, in the best-seller realm, to which kingdom even the most non-material writer somehow aspires.

CHAPTER 19

RADIO AND TELEVISION

IT is a good idea for a beginner to have a shot at writing for radio or television, not because the chances of acceptance are high (on the contrary they are probably lower for the beginner than in any other type of writing) but because, by trying his hand at different ventures, the new writer may find the specialism in which he is most likely to do well.

Radio networks are shortly to be increased in England and this will provide further opportunities for the writer with aural as opposed to visual imagination.

The best way to succeed in radio is to study the *Radio Times* and Local Radio programmes to see what is being produced each week, and then to attempt to write for a particular slot, such as the Short Story, Woman's Hour, Talks or radio Drama.

If you write a talk and are asked up to record it, practise on a tape recorder first, or ask some kind person (relative?) to listen to your reading of the MS. and possibly to give you advice on how to improve it. If your script is particularly good and your voice not suitable for radio, a reader will be found for you at the studios. Sometimes your reading of your own script is so lamentable it will merit the thumbs down sign altogether. My first radio script for the B.B.C. ended in this way. I had written a talk and was asked up to record it. Within the talk was some mimicked dialogue, including Cockney. The B.B.C. did not like my reading, but did like the Cockney dialogue. The producer asked me if I could do some Cockney scripts. I was young and inexperienced then and didn't think I could manage to write them and said so. (Moral: a professional writer can write *anything*!) My talk was not used. I did, however, later write to the B.B.C. and ask for expenses. They explained it was not their policy to reimburse unsuccessful writers for their attendance, but surprisingly, paid up. (Re-read the Chapter on *Letters*.)

Not until many years later did I attempt another talk, by which time a new producer was in charge. But this time I had learnt my lesson and spent hours practising the script. People with naturally interesting, dramatic or pleasant voices need not bother rehearsing in this way, but those with a 'flat' voice can learn to alter their pitch and pace.

The talk was very successful. But though I spent two years overseas as a script writer in the 'English by Radio' series, I have not been tempted to write again for the radio in England. This is not because of the intense competition. I just have the feeling . . . and it is only a feeling . . . which doesn't exist for me in any other writing field at all . . . that knowing somebody in the organization helps. In other spheres of writing my experience has led me to believe that you are judged solely on what you produce, by the quality of your work alone, not in any way by who or what you are (save of course in the case of columns written by experts: sportsmen, gardeners, musicians, doctors, etc.). Your work is the only thing that matters.

Furthermore, radio and television have this tremendous disadvantage for the unknown writer: that they are a near monopoly. If your work is unacceptable to the B.B.C. or independent television companies, where else can you find a market? By contrast, there are at least one hundred and fifty publishers operating in London and if a novel or non-fiction book is turned down by one, you still have one hundred and forty-nine further chances. And there are at least 4,000 magazine editors, one of whom you may, with luck, delude into thinking you are an unrecognized genius.

On the other hand, the young beginner with no published work at all, has nothing to lose, except time, and much to gain by attempting the challenging media of TV and sound.

He can learn techniques as he progresses, for TV and radio are still so new compared with the world of print, that the innovator may have as much to contribute as the experienced professional.

Intending playwrights are often advised to submit a preliminary letter or synopsis or plot together with specimen pages of drama for a play. I would never do this myself except for an adaptation of a novel or short story. In these two cases it may happen that an adaptation has already been made or is scheduled for production, and a synopsis will save you much fruitless work. But otherwise there is no point in doing so, for no copyright exists in ideas. If a newspaper or magazine editor likes your ideas, however 'unknown' your name may be, he will often pay for the ideas alone . . . even if he can't use your write-up. Ideas by unknowns may be similarly paid for in the radio or TV world, but I have not heard of it being done.

It seems far better to submit the whole or major part of any play. If the whole doesn't suit, it's hardly likely that a part will be acceptable, and the person who has the talent to write an acceptable (part) script, isn't likely to baulk at doing the whole job. Writing a play rarely takes up as much time as the writing of a novel, and the whole play has to be finished some time. Why not as you go along?

Because TV and radio have a family audience, subjects of general human interest are the most acceptable, but controversial themes are welcomed for later 'slots'. Talks must be written as colloquially as possible. The producer at the B.B.C. studios gave me this very helpful advice about radio talks: to write as if you were chatting to a friend or neighbour about some subject of very real interest to both of you.

In TV your chance of acceptances, if you are a beginner, will be restricted if your play features a large cast or has many changes of scenery. Two people on a park bench, in a telephone booth, or one or two rooms of a house, are economical settings for TV scripts, but ringing the changes must be a challenge to a writer's ingenuity.

Don't worry overmuch about writing detailed camera instructions. If the producer likes and accepts your play, he will add his own camera directions later. Set out the dialogue so that it is easily distinguishable from sound or visual effects.

Aural and visual media have different advantages. In TV a glance or gesture can convey the equivalent of several lines of dialogue or descriptive writing: a single shot almost as much meaning as a full length novel. As an example of the economy of film, consider *Compulsion* directed by Roman Polanski. From an almost unbearably slow opening we move to the point where a young heroine's incipient insanity culminates, because of the presence of her sister's lover in their shared flat, in two murders. The horror of the murders is emphasized not only by the complete innocence of one of the victims, but the way chance has led them both to their death.

When the sister returns to the London flat from a holiday with her lover, the discovery of the first corpse causes her to scream hysterically. Soon the landing is full of people. They gradually filter out from flats where previously in the film only one person has ever been seen before. The lover comes in, picks up the senseless body of the beautiful young murderer, and the camera now pans round the flat showing the knot of gossiping people, a half eaten biscuit crumbled on the floor, the ornaments, the debris, the ticking clock . . . and a family photograph.

The camera focuses slowly on the photograph in which the young murderer can be seen as a schoolgirl. She is looking at an older man who appears to be her father . . . a photograph, it seems, such as might be found in any old family album. But the camera directs its beam on the schoolgirl's face, and then the eyes, so that gradually the magnification becomes frightening. And as we, the viewers, watch the child's askance, suspicious (?) glance at her father's (?) image, we wonder, if this is where the seeds of madness were first sown. The child's eye grows larger until it is blurred into a terrifying nothingness, and the film ends. This shot of the schoolgirl's face has in it a touch of genius. The director achieves this distinction not only because of the quality of his ideas, but because he knows so precisely how to use the medium in which he works to express those ideas.

This is the great challenge for the creative writer on TV or radio, that settings may be anywhere, events happen in any world, past, present or to come, because time and place can be indicated by sight or sound alone.

Appendices

ACROSS AT THE RUBBISH ROOM
DOOR AND THE GRIMY IN-
TERNAL WINDOW. HE IS
FRIGHTENED.

8. INT. RUBBISH ROOM. NIGHT.

BOTH KEVIN AND MIKE AT THE
WINDOW.

KEVIN: Hc knows we're here!

MIKE: So?

MIKE PULLS A COSH FROM HIS
POCKET. KEVIN STARES AT THE
COSH WILD-EYED. IT'S THE
FIRST TIME HE'S SEEN IT.
MIKE SMILES.

Appendix III

NOTES ON WRITING PLAYS FOR TELEVISION

Advantages. The camera is mobile. This means that the writer can be more economical with words in a TV script than with a story, or stage play. Descriptions are unnecessary. The camera reveals all. On a theatre stage an actor may have to speak a few lines of dialogue to convey a reaction or emotion which in a TV studio could be expressed by a mere change of facial expression. Directions as to what the characters may be feeling are useful, but *not* what the camera can see. Leave that to the producer.

Expense. As noted earlier in this book, your chances of acceptance will be reduced if your play involves the use of elaborate sets or expensive equipment. Try to make the action take place in not more than two main (built up) sets. Use your ingenuity in devising meeting places for your characters that do not mean much change of scenery: a telephone booth, park bench, balcony, street corner, small section of a room. When you are famous, you can demand what you like. Keep your characters down to three at most. TV is not the wide screen which reproduces so well the quality of grandeur in a landscape or the heroism and futility of a battle in which hundreds are engaged.

In your script, allow time for any changes of scenery or costume. If your character appears at the end of one scene in a particular place or in a particular costume which has to be changed for his next appearance, try to avoid having him at the beginning of the next scene. If you introduce an interval. ... End of Act One ... end it on an up-beat which will make the viewer continue on the (commercial) channel in spite of the advertisements intervening.

Subject. Almost all subjects are today acceptable. But you are not writing for a mass group audience though your viewers may number many millions. The audience is always an individual one made up mostly of small family groups in their own homes. This means that sincerity of theme, emotion, and character are vital. Select subjects of general human interest. Writers of historical drama are usually commissioned. Contemporary themes get a more favourable reception than costume plays.

Synopses. Send a complete play rather than a synopsis, unless you have some prior knowledge that the B.B.C. or I.T.V. companies have an interest in your work. In this case give a synopsis of at least 300 words, with your name, address and phone number, the type (i.e. into which 'slot' you are hoping your play will fit or the kind of play it is . . . contemporary, historical) the length and the title. A title, even only a tentative one that you may decide to alter later on, safeguards the copyright in your synopsis. Enclose a stamped addressed envelope. Your script should be acknowledged within a few weeks, and a decision for acceptance or rejection made a few weeks after that.

Do not try *adaptations* without a query. You will be wasting your time. Most adaptations are carried out by staff writers employed by the television companies. If however you are in the fortunate position (unlikely for a beginner) of having some especial connection with an author who will give you permission to adapt his work, you are in a very favourable position to negotiate terms with the TV companies.

Queries. Queries are useful only for obtaining up-to-date information on work currently being sought by TV companies. This can alternatively be provided by a good agent, who receives it direct, or by writers joining the Writers' Guild of Great Britain, which receives market information as it becomes available. A useful booklet is *Writing for the B.B.C.* This sums up the Corporation's requirements in television and radio.

Finally: Keep watching to see the kind of plays currently being produced. This is your market, and you must know what is being bought and sold in this market if you are to succeed with your own sales. Send your script clearly typed, with the self-addressed stamped envelope, to any of the TV companies listed in the *Writers' and Artists' Year Book* or to Head of Script Department, B.B.C. Television Centre, White City, W.12. Then sit back and think how wonderful it is to be a dramatist at last.

Index

Accuracy, 18, 58
Action, 22, 88
Adventure stories, 99–100
Agents, Literary, 91–2
Aims, 11, 45–53
Angle, 24
Appeal, 24
Art work, 92
Articles
  Advertising, 84–7
  Children's, 89
  General, 83
  'How to . . .', 72
  Religious, 76
  Topical, 71, 74, 78
  Travel, 72–3, 78
  Specialist, 73–4, 81–3

Beginnings, 30–4
British Museum, 27
Business communication, 57–61
  accuracy, 58
  intelligibility, 57

Children's Page, 90
Comics, 89
Competition in children's market, 88
Crime stories, 99–100

Dialects, 69
Dialogue, 52, 113–15
Dictating machine, 16
Dictionary, 15
Discipline, 21, 88
Drama script, notes on, Appendix I,
  sample, Appendix I

Educational market, 101–2
Endings, 30–4
Examinations
  General Certificate of Education,
    62–5
  Banking Diploma Examinations, 63
  Higher National Diplomas, 67
  Theses, 70

Facts, 23
  lack of, 49
Feature articles, 71–4
Film rights, 90–1
First British Serial Rights, 90, 91

Geffrye Museum, 28
Grammar, 14

Hampton Court, 28
House Journals, 60

Ideas
  Finding, 25–9
  Selling, 22–4
  Starting, 19–21
Idioms, 69
Inactivity, 25
Incidents, 97
Inspiration, 25–6
Interviews, 76–7

Juvenile market, 88–92

Kate Greenaway Medal, 92

Letters, 40–4
  appealing, 40

basic points of, 42
denouncing, 45
placating, 40
stating, 43
tone of, 40
Literature, English, definition of, 65

Magazines
Children's, 90
Confession, 98–9
Women's, 98
Works, 60
Manuscripts,
Handwritten, 14
Typed, 14
Marketing, art of, 48
Markets,
lack of, 47
wrong, 47
Memoranda, 59
Minutes, 58
Motivation, 25, 45–6, 97

Novels, 93
religious themes, 79–80

Observation, 25–6
Organization of work, 17
Output, 19

Paperback revolution, 88
Passion in writing, 23, 72
Personal file, 16
Persistence, 16–17
Plots, 97
Press clippings, 16
Public libraries, 16
Public Records Office, 26
Publishers' lists, 104

Radio, talks, 106–7
technique, 108
recording for, 106
Readers' needs, 22

Reference books, 15
Benn's Newspaper Directory, 15
British Rate and Data, 15
Business Surveys Ltd, Source List, 16
Guinness Book of Records, 16, 102
Little Red Book Guide, 15
Modern English Usage, 15, 48, 90, 102
Newspaper Press Directory, 61
Roget's Thesaurus, 102
Willing's Press Guide, 15, 61
Writers and Artists' Year Book, 15, 20,
48, 73, 90
Writer's Market, 15
Writer's Notebook, 20
Reporting meetings, 77–8
Reports, 59
Reward titles, 79
Romance, 23

Short stories, 79, 87, 91, 97–8, 106
Similes, 52
Slant, 24
Specialism, 73–4, 86, 106
Specimen chapters, 51, 93, 104
Spelling, 14
Statistics, 52
Sterility of ideas, 25
Style, lack of, 47–8
poor, 49
Subject, wrong, 47–8
Syndicates, 90
Synopses, 93, 104–5, 107, 117
Syntax, 15

Tabulated matter, 49
Talent, 17
Tape recorder, 16
Tate Gallery, 28
Television
layout of scripts, Appendices I and II
scripts for, 108
technique, 107–8, Appendix III
Test questions, 52
Textbooks, 101–2
Timing, 49, 74

Titles, 35-7
  alliteration, 36
  allusion, 37
  appeal, 35
  brevity, 35
  contrast, 37
  humour, 37
  repetition, 37
  rhyme, 37
  rhythm, 37
  slant, 35
  true, 35
Travel articles, 72, 78, 86

Victoria and Albert Museum, 27
Vocabulary, 14

Words, number of, 105
Works magazines, 60